"Having tried to pretzel herself to fit inher rejecting the lot in disgust, Jean Waight unexpectedly finds treasure behind door number three—inclusive, non-patriarchal, and liberating. Weaving an astonishing tapestry of canoeing, scholarship, mountaintop experience, and a very human set of fellow travelers, she brings us on her adventure forging a new identity. And a new understanding of Christianity emerges: that there is *always* a place for God in a rapidly changing world as long as we accept that we are continual works in progress."

—**Cami Ostman**, co-editor of *Beyond Belief: The Secret Lives of Women in Extreme Religions*

"Jean Waight made room on her canoe and let me travel along her faith journey, and it was a most enjoyable ride. Many times along the way I was heartened and encouraged by Waight's words and perspectives. I felt like I was not alone on my own faith journey, but in good company. This book is a must read for any progressive Christian, or anyone interested in a fresh perspective on what a Christian life can look like. I wholeheartedly recommend this book, and I look forward to more from Waight."

—**Priscilla Goins**, author of *Early Bird Special: An Oak Grove Story*

"This is indeed a wild ride on the rapids. In a mix of personal reflection, metaphor, scholarly discourse, and just plain good storytelling, Jean Waight takes your mind to new places and shows you the power of faith in action. She shifts the very foundation of religious and philosophical thought for most people raised in traditional thinking; a gentle push to start your own journey."

—**Kristin Noreen**, author of *On Silver Wings: A Life Reconstructed*

The River Beyond the Dam

The River Beyond the Dam

Shooting the Rapids of Progressive Christianity

A Memoir

Jean L. Waight

ILLUSTRATIONS BY
Emily Wagnitz

RESOURCE *Publications* · Eugene, Oregon

THE RIVER BEYOND THE DAM
Shooting the Rapids of Progressive Christianity: A Memoir

Resource Publications
An Imprint of Wipf and Stock Publishers
199 W. 8th Ave., Suite 3
Eugene, OR 97401

www.wipfandstock.com

PAPERBACK ISBN: 978-1-6667-6772-8
HARDCOVER ISBN: 978-1-6667-6773-5
EBOOK ISBN: 978-1-6667-6774-2

03/30/23

Chapter illustrations copyright Emily Wagnitz.

Bible verses cited are from the Revised Standard Version (RSV) or the New Revised Standard Version (NRS) unless otherwise noted.

For Helen McLeod, in memoriam

And for Bill, always

Jean Waight

Contents

CONTENTS

Acknowledgments

Applause to artist Emily Wagnitz. I can't imagine a better collaborator. She took sketchy ideas and turned them into the evocative illustrations you see in the chapters. Her talents are many, and she helped me enjoy bringing this project to life.

To my earliest readers, Armand Larive and Amory Peck, my immense gratitude for seeing the value in a manuscript that hadn't found its form yet. A big thank you to each of the subsequent readers who nudged me to improvements and who heartened me when they found resonances: Victoria Reeve, Chris Straker, Kristin Noreen, Priscilla Goins, Abbie Breckbill, Lisa Dailey, Judith Shantz, and my thought partner on the river-and-dam motif, my dear friend Laura Velm.

To my editor, Anna Lawson, my thanks for her wide-ranging experience, deep appreciation for churches that nurture, and her humor. Her help was invaluable.

To Mark Schofield, Krista Hunter, and Mark Glickman, who graciously shared their stories and thoughts that so enriched this journey-story, my thanks. To my beloved sister, Julie Edwards, with whom I re-lived and recalled our time in Panama. And bottom-of-my heart gratitude to the pastors and members of First Congregational Church of Bellingham who welcomed me into their flotilla of boats and never quit paddling.

Thanks to the Red Wheelbarrow Writers association, for all you have taught me about writing, especially Laura Kalpakian, Cami Ostman, and Drue Robinson, and for the group's collegial, companionable, writerly friendship. Thanks as well to Sean Dwyer for running a regular open mic, and to Village Books for providing their venue to wholeheartedly support writers and readers.

Thank you to Wipf and Stock Publishers for permission to use Michael Coffey's poem, "Palm or Passion: Wave or Particle," from *Mystery*

Without Rhyme or Reason: Poetic Reflections on the Revised Common Lectionary, 2015.

Last, I'll never forget the wonderful folks of the Paddle Trails Canoe Club who so long ago taught life lessons as well as canoeing skills.

1: An Unlikely Quest

My exhilaration evaporated at the sight of the broad boulder dead ahead. I yelled to Bill, who steered from the stern of our canoe, but he didn't hear me over the frothy roar. Twisting in my seat, I jabbed my paddle in a frantic, angry arrow and re-aimed my shout backward: "Boulder!" He still didn't understand, nor see through the obscuring turmoil. Time running out, I bent to one of the few evasive maneuvers available to the bow and rehearsed the mantra we'd been taught: If you dump and are swept down river, "*Keep* your *feet up.*"

When I look back on my river canoeing years, I remember our panics and our marital tussles. I remember strained shoulders and stretched elbows from hauling our first canoe, a too-heavy decked model. I remember a dump in water so frigid my chest seized and I shot straight up, a Polaris missile. The awful sound of an elephant's trumpet, but in reverse. This must have been before I got a wetsuit. But my canoeing memories also include the local paddling club we joined, friendly people with a common purpose, patient and willing to teach us.

With their class for newbies, and their coaching, we had many joyful outings on the rivers up and down Northwest Washington. One day we even were able to perch on a standing wave. We held our paddles jubilantly overhead and surfed in place. I don't know what shaped the riverbed at that spot, but whatever it was kicked up a wave that folded over on itself and stopped the forward flow there. I only know sitting atop this wave was a gas.

Despite the rougher moments, river canoeing has always sat easy on my mind—they are memories I'm glad to have. Even those tussles between bow and stern got laughed off over a beer.

Not sitting so easy on my mind was another part of my past, my years in Protestant Christian churches. It's not that I thought of those days often. But it's funny how the past doesn't always resolve neatly into one's life story but can stay tucked on a back shelf, like canned goods long past their pull date and maybe even bulging ominously. My strains and pains in the churches of my youth and the memory of Christian strictures on women still nettled me occasionally, even decades after I left. A mere glimpse of devotional books in a store window could make me flinch. I would think about how, for the devout, the honeyed devotionals held in place the status quo—"Trust and obey, for there's no other way. . ."

Unlike the friendly group of experienced paddlers who accepted me fully, the adult Christians I remembered while a sophomore in high school in the Panama Canal Zone seemed to be not with me, really, but only acting a role. A handful of the Panama Christian youth group became good friends, regular kids who could be teased for ordering gravy on their French fries (in the muggy hot tropics, no less) at the Balboa military base hangout, and who got weak in the knees like I did for such pop songs as "Unchained Melody." Having a community of friends there is a sweet memory. But as far as Wednesday night prayer meetings and soulful witness and Sunday services and Christian counseling went, I didn't want to remember my church years at all and was sure I'd never go back.

I could see that men's elevation above women wasn't necessarily a huge prize for them, either. Men were required to fall in line, unquestioning, behind a leader. Neither men nor women were entitled to own their own minds. Moreover, in the decades after I left, from what I could see there hadn't been much updating in Christianity's received cosmology since medieval times. It was as if Christianity asked modern people to return through the mists of time to when medicine was blood-letting, and ragged men pulled wooden-wheeled carts along rough cobblestones, singing out a tired dirge, "Bring out your dead." I'm sorry. That was facetious. But after my sister Rosemary joined an arch-conservative Lutheran church in Tacoma, Washington, complete with it's own private school, I made the mistake of taking Mom to a museum, or the wrong museum. Mom spent a lot of time with Rosemary in those days. In the museum, the first exhibits Mom and I came to described evolution. Gads.

In my Christian youth I tried to accept doctrines we were warned off from examining. I just couldn't in the end pray my way around either my gut or my brain. To me, doctrines should be something to take seriously, and be ready to pledge myself to. I couldn't stay because I couldn't perform the theological acrobatics. Nor could I ignore doctrine, simply sliding into and out of a clubbish argot at the door as if it were a member's jacket or a secret handshake. Religion had to work not only inside a church but out in the world. Besides, doctrines have consequences, and there was the real rub.

Much of my youthful objection stemmed from a deeply troubling first principle in Christian teachings going back to the third century: that humans are born with a bad nature. A bad nature. Not good and bad, both. Just bad. This teaching didn't come from Jesus, and didn't come from Judaism, as I discuss in a later chapter. I carry a great sadness for that doctrine's harm on generations of children subject to corporal punishment, and the brutalizing of (typically) women teachers in both religious and secular schools who carried out this punishment, their beliefs and their orders overriding their basic instincts. I am so grateful that innate badness was simply not what my mother's love taught me. She taught by her actions that I was good. So did Genesis, I thought, where it said God made us and called us good (even if we might slip up).

I know there are Christian adherents who don't believe all they are told to believe—I wouldn't have been born if my mother, a religious woman, had accepted a doctrine that consigned unbaptized babies to Hell. A man who believed that asked her to marry him. She liked him, but she loved babies deeply, and his beliefs, to use an old theater expression, tore it. She married my father instead, a man I'm guessing who didn't talk religious beliefs at all. I know that many women—Black, white, and Latina—have found strength through their Christian faith. Men, too, of course, though a little differently. Kathleen Norris, a religion teacher and poet who explored feminist theology before she could consider returning to church herself, came to a similar acknowledgment of "a central paradox of the Christian faith: that while the religion has often been used as an agent of women's oppression, it also has had a remarkable ability to set women free."[1] However, as a middle-class

---

1. Norris, *Amazing Grace*, 135. Her entire chapter, "Conversion: The Feminist Impasse," is still well worth reading.

white woman full of promise, I experienced a kind of religion that did more to sit on my chest, curtailing what was tantalizingly in sight—life's fullness—than it ever did to provide me strength.

I don't want to suggest that my childhood and teen experience of Christianity was any kind of a fringe or abusive experience. Even in high school I knew about fringe groups, ever since the day I was over at a girl-friend's house after school. My friend Barb's father had been rendered quadriplegic in an accident, and was having prospective caregivers come to the house for interviews. I answered the door for Barb, and a steely-eyed matron barely said hello before, right there on the stoop, she told me sternly that I'd better get saved and mend my ways or I was going to Hell. I asked her how she knew all that just by one look at me. Easy. I was wearing slacks, she said, not a skirt. *That* was fringe.

No, I really didn't want to remember my church years. I'm pro-equal-ity and science-oriented—my master's degree in sociology, completed in my forties, focused on the American myth—even enshrined in the trap-pings of social science theory—that we have a meritocracy. I could stay in my secular humanist cocoon, and I was prepared to do so. I wasn't really hurting for meaning in my life, even though I'd not had children to invest myself in. I found meaning in people—long friendships, marriage to Bill, our extended families—and in great, transporting literature and in music. And, yes, in doing for others outside of family and friends, when oppor-tunity presented itself. I was never going to be a saint, either the selfless or any other kind. But it felt good to have used my management position to help develop the careers of others. And good to have added my bit of original research to the sociology of inequality. I was also glad I'd been a Campfire leader and a Big Sister.

I jockeyed with Bill and longtime friends and boaters Chris and Bill and Peter and Mary for a view at a chain link fence, the wind whipping up from the gorge below to lift our hats and hair. It was May of 2011 and we were looking down a precipice into a deep and ancient river canyon. We stood on the site of a dam demolition project on the Elwha River above Port An-geles, Washington. The work, the largest dam removal in U.S. history, was to begin that September, slowly and carefully, piece by 1913 piece. The dam we saw from the fence was the lower dam. A larger dam hid from our view further upriver. After thirty years of discussion, the two dams had been declared necessary no more.

One problem for the project was the huge load of stalled sediment that would charge forward to be sluiced out by a freed-up Elwha. The sediment waiting to rumble included rock and gravel sloughed off the Olympic Mountains where the river originates. We stood a while and laughed in the wind, and looked down from our dizzying height at rock walls and the water flinging its spray up the canyon at us.

From the fence, though we were practically on top of the dam, trees and brush kept us from a view of the artificial lake penned-up behind the dam. I tried to imagine paddling in that lake, if somehow I were plunked down on it. Or if I lived on that side of the dam. From my imaginary spot on this perched lake, I wouldn't see the river beyond the dam, and its flow, and I might be unaware that the lake was held in place by concrete. Perhaps I wouldn't know of the forceful engineering, and over time, the patching, layering on, the reinforcing. The lake, held back in this way, would seem unchanging. And so would my paddling options. It would simply be "the way it is."

Bill and I were back the next year and watched with glee as the river fell with a joyful noise through the breached and partially removed dam. Almost free-running now, the water tonnage churned along rocks where the river resumed its grounded flow toward the waiting estuary. This year it was as if the power of the river respectfully nodded to the previous power of the dam and the work it had done for the city. And then prepared to say good-bye, and resume its ancient purpose.

Returning the third spring, both dams gone, we thrilled to the full re-wilding of this precious Elwha River. Upriver from the narrow canyon that once had been so enticing as a dam site, native plantings in protective blue sleeves took hold on new river banks that long had been under water. We could see the plantings from the hiking trail we took to Goblins Gate. And down at the estuary, salmon nosed their way back, the scent of life in the air rather than the smell of dank concrete.

It was before I started dam-watching that my life underwent a major passage. In 2004, my job was ending, and that was going to leave a hole I didn't know what to do with. I was working in communications and community relations at Group Health Cooperative, and one of my duties was liaison to an advisory group made up of astute member-consumers from a four-county area. I liked the group, mostly retirees, and in particular, I liked Dick Covington, a Bellingham, Washington, man who took a stint as chair.

I was drawn to his relaxed warmth and easy sense of humor, the way he deadpanned a punchline you didn't see coming. I learned he was active with a local organization called Inter-Faith Coalition, which sounded interesting—many faith communities somehow working together, if that was even possible. Asking, I learned that he was a member of the First Congregational Church of Bellingham. Somehow I couldn't picture him singing the insistent childhood rouser seared into my synapses, about the joy! joy! joy! joy! down in my heart, moreover, declaring I had a peace passing all understanding. Who has that kind of peace? This was a sticky residue of the ghost of religion past, a song I'd felt pushed to sing in churches of my youth, whether or not I felt it. What a way to make a child feel like a fraud even before she knows what fraud is?

Around this same time I was in my kitchen up to my elbows in August's harvest bounty. I could scarcely believe what Bill was willing to pay for a box of tomatoes that were, by local farm Joe's Garden's own labeling, "scratch and dent," and looked near to being compost. When I plunged into trimming, cutting out the bad—there was actual blue mold where a few had cracked open, their thin skin unable to contain their ripeness—I sniffed and rarely had to discard or cut away deeper. These tomatoes would indeed work for sauce. They actually smelled really good. Stirring the first batch of tasty sauce, I fleetingly wondered why someone like Dick would attend church. But I didn't burn any brain cells on this thought.

Burbling through my cooking chores was a different thought—a rumination about what I was going to do with my new freedom from the job. I would miss many generous and smart colleagues, along with work I believed in. But freedom from work, even with a belt worn tighter, had me hoping for some kind of healing. I thought mostly about physical strengthening, but I had to admit I wasn't doing all that great psychologically. To be sure, I had my long-time friends, dear and much admired, though, since our move to Bellingham, many of them now were a hundred miles away. I had various comforts as needed: travel trips, favorite foods, yoga, and of course, my good (second) marriage to Bill. I'd certainly had my headaches and anxieties with my work and career, and some relationship problems, like with my mother as I moved through my thirties. I didn't want to be labeled, but various stresses and lows had me looking for help from time to time—I went to counseling, hypnosis, medications, yoga, meditation, and I did workbooks—Hugh Prather's and Julia Cameron's. Still, even if I felt too easily knocked sideways,

I was prepared to just go forward and see what my next life chapter would bring. I started art lessons, very enjoyable.

And yet.

A few months relaxing at home, and painting, and I saw my world shrinking. I was missing *something*. Music told me so. I knew when Mozart or Beethoven could bring tears to my eyes from some kind of unresolved deep emotion, and more contemporary music (Joni Mitchell!) could collapse me or get me up to dance. I knew I had liked singing hymns in a large group, the thrumming in my chest, the warmth all around me. Certainly in church I had sung words that felt false; still, the melodies stayed with me. I had loved singing the alto part that harmonized thrillingly with the soprano, sometimes tilting my head toward a soprano to really hear us together. And the men's voices grounded and deepened the swell. I didn't have much of a singing voice, but in a large group that didn't matter. Old melodies that I wasn't aware were classical or folk tunes supported the hymns I remembered, and I loved them, stirringly beautiful as they still are.

What had my friend Dick found at First Congregational? Was it just a social life, a club like Kiwanis for extroverted do-gooders? Was it, perhaps, about providing familiar comfort to aging folks? Or about gentling the young, as in parents looking for ethics training, whether or not these parents wanted religion for themselves.

I wondered what Dick's Congregational church was up to. I might just go satisfy my curiosity. I didn't really expect it was radically different—different would be a church that wasn't exalting men over women, didn't require me to believe in original sin (especially as blamed on the woman), didn't proclaim we are to subdue the Earth, didn't shut down questions, or align itself with hatred of LGBTQ folks. A bit of do-goodism layered on would not be enough for me. A really different kind of Christian church, much like a good canoe, could withstand scraping in the river shallows. Its members would live their belief that religion is better with others by your side. And have no hard boundaries pitted against and holding back the world. This kind of church was not just a tall order but inconceivable to me.

But perhaps there was the merest chance that a church might at least somehow ease me into greater peace of mind with myself and the world. Unlikely. I didn't expect anything.

Still, maybe it wouldn't hurt to visit. See what I could see.

2: First Visit

I made my first visit to First Congregational Church of Bellingham on a fine Sunday in early 2005. Sadly, Dick was very ill by this time, and he wasn't there to greet me. I was on my own. This first time I didn't want any pressure, and hoped only to observe as invisibly as possible. So I pushed to the back of my closet, past my usual denim and plaids, for something in a Bellingham business style—not tightly tailored like somebody important, nor in the latest style, just what might be called classic. There wasn't much in my closet that could be termed fashion-forward in any case. For me now, fashion is too much work to keep up, not to mention the money that I'd much rather spend on good food. That's age for you.

Parking my Camry, I now saw up close the large church building I'd passed by so often on Cornwall Avenue. Somehow the light gray church building had read in my mind as a pale blue—maybe it was the sky that lent some of its color. The overall size of the clapboarded building broke down into many gracefully joined parts, angles, windows, and gables. Just past a peaceful bit of garden with a polished stone bench, I mounted the broad concrete steps to the wide open French doors, and was greeted by a couple stationed beyond the cloak room. They stuck gently to their wall, not stepping out to glad-hand anyone. Evidently they were the official greeters this

Sunday; they wore name badges, shook my hand and said good morning and welcome, and smiled at me.

I found myself in an open area that felt like a courtyard. This interior was pleasing, gracious, with open lines of sight to the other entrance, and through glass to a large hall on the right and the Sanctuary on the left. I was by turns wary and open. Maybe I was like a cat wary of being grabbed at, that wants to observe and take the temperature before sidling up to a pant leg. Yet curious, or what was the point? Several clusters of middle-aged people, twos and threes, stood talking, and although these people looked comfortably well-off, they were not ostentatious—I wasn't seeing bejeweled necks, thank goodness; though a few were dressed in current fashion, others wore perennial dress clothes or looked to be in the same garb they wore everyday. A glance or two lit on me, with warm smiles that let me be. I was immediately more comfortable than I expected to be.

Not seeing anyone I knew, I headed into the Sanctuary, where a tranquil usher handed me the bulletin for the day's service. I took a seat in a back row. The banks of pews arrayed themselves a fan shape. I liked that this largest of rooms wasn't the old two banks of straight-ahead pews. In the fan arrangement you could see each other better—not just the backs of heads. Through an open window came soft sounds of cars rolling by on dry pavement. The space around me vaulted high and airy. Honey-colored laminated fir beams spanned the width far above our heads, the beams' bottom edge curvature hinting at the arcs of bridges, thickening where they tied into soft yellow walls. Dark bronzy organ pipes rose from the wall at center-left. A round table held pride of place at center front, blond wood carved in pillowy interlocking representations. Silk banners fluttered softly behind the pulpit to the right, telling a story in gorgeous blues, greens, and yellows. I could see that this space of understated beauty could display a changing array of decorations.

The tall cross at center front—up the risers into the chancel—commanded my eye. But it gave off a different emotional charge than any I'd seen. Not a literal wooden replica, as I'd seen so many times in churches I'd attended or been in for memorial services. No, this cross was solid art glass, narrow, elongated to rise maybe eighteen feet into the vaulted space, the surface textured like rivulets of rain. Still more remarkable was its brightness; its depth penetrated the wall all the way to the outside, letting in light, like a window. Then I saw that my first impression wasn't quite right. Faint light also bathed the edges of a suede-brown plinth that the cross was set into, the whole thing set a bit away from the back wall. There must be a tall window hidden behind the plinth to daylight its edges and the glass cross. I wasn't a fan of typical Christian emphasis on the crucifixion. Still, at this moment I appreciated the symbolism I could see here, that the Christian cross could let in light. The Sanctuary had no stained glass window aiming for beauty or commanding awe or glorifying the church. Only light. I wondered what this congregation made of their artistic cross.

As people streamed in, I didn't want my fastened gaze to attract attention, so I pulled a hymnal from the rack on the pew in front of me, intending to busy myself with my bulletin previewing the hymns for the day. On impulse I turned to the table of contents and scanned down to see what I would recognize, and frankly, what I might find to hold against this simple, well-meaning book. In the middle of the alphabet, I saw no listing for "Onward Christian Soldiers." That one was a litmus test for me, because it sees enemies and battle everywhere, rather than neighbors and peacemaking. So far so good, and the volume hadn't scorched my hand. I would one day dredge up my teenage memories of the church in the Panama Canal Zone and its association with "Christian soldiers." But for today, I needed that hymn to not be there.

That morning, as I scanned the contents page to the bottom, a title jumped out: "We Are Marching." I pounced, flipping to the page. The hymnal lay open in my hand, staying flat just as you'd want, the pages smooth with a quality coating. From childhood piano lessons I could read music, at least somewhat, and I could mentally hear that this was no sturdy song to be sung dutifully. A touch of syncopation gave it a buoyancy, and indeed the next words after "we are marching" were "in the light of God." Here was the image of light again, the words reinforcing the visual of the glass cross. I liked that, and it felt like this emphasis was not accidental. Rivers sparkle with light.

Another hymn spoke of no one standing alone. Even in my critical, cautious attitude I had to admit that sounded good. After all, if you can't feel part of a united group in church, with lots of folks who have your back, where can you? Continuing my quick scan, I saw Beethoven's "Hymn to Joy," which I'd known as "Ode to Joy." And also "For the Beauty of the Earth," an elegiac piece I'd loved. I just had time to notice a hymn in Spanish and wonder what this assembly did with *that*, when the big-throated bell sounded in the tower above us. Rung by hand, the bell stuttered as if a child was over his depth trying to haul the pull-rope. Likely that was the case—children, I would learn, were regularly invited to serve as bell-ringers.

The pastor opened the service with an elaborate welcome—everyone is welcome, he said, no matter who you are or where you are on life's journey. By now I was all ears. I set the hymnal beside me on the blue upholstery, the book's gold embossed title face up. It had tentatively passed my test even before we sang. I didn't know it then, but this *New Century Hymnal*, published by Pilgrim Press in 1995, purposely honors both male and female images of God, according to the archives of the United Church of Christ.

That day I heard no hammering from the pulpit about being a believer. I was glad, of course. But also, even on that early day in my quest, there seemed something odd about making belief the centerpiece of a religion. I thought of the vast difference between inspirational literature, so abstract and ephemeral, and the workbooks I'd spent time with that were all about practice, about applying insights and working them down deep. What if the question, "Are you a believer or a nonbeliever?" is the wrong question? Years on, I learned how much I'd thought was fixed in Christianity from its start had in fact changed a lot over the centuries, and not for the better. Robin R. Meyers wrote in *Saving Jesus from the Church* that it was only after the Reformation, far removed from the time of Christian origins, that "the meaning of 'orthodoxy' shifted from 'correct worship' to 'right belief.'"[1] It was further downstream on my river journey that I encountered this Robin Meyers fellow, and when I did it was like getting the giggles in a class three rapids. This Christian tenet that really doesn't *serve* many like me hadn't been there in the beginning after all.

---

1. Meyers, *Saving Jesus*, 37.

3: A River in Motion

I n this new century, it may seem an odd time for any atheist or rote
Christian or former Christian—or anyone taking a solo path—to take
a fresh look at church. Church is part of a waning era, it seems, hardly
relevant for today. Worse, certain American evangelicals have lost themselves in White Christian Nationalism. A political cult of the strayed—
how else can Christian Nationalism be seen, when the loudest white
evangelical Christian leaders go out of their way to defend powerful men
whose crimes have caught up with them, and worse, viciously denigrate
the victims who have raised their voices?

But this church, here on the ground in Bellingham, Washington, was
clearly not of the same species as churches with the top-down, rigid, we'll-
tell-you-what-to-believe and by the way you-were-born-a-miserable-sin-
ner, known as the old-time religion. So I went back. And then I went back
again. Bill began to ask on Sundays if I was going to *church*, with a needling,
hard "ch," which he tried to soften with a big teasing grin. He would typically look up from the sports section of the Sunday paper with expectant
blue eyes that told me he was paying close attention to my reply. My leaving
seemed a violation of our long-standing and deeply pleasing Sunday habit,
that of lingering over coffee and the oven pancake that he likes to make on

Sunday, with a sliced pear and blueberries and maple syrup, accompanied by music from our collection of LP vinyl platters.

One Sunday, I saw his forehead creasing as he watched me head to the coat closet yet again and he asked, yet again, "Going to church?" This time I felt his unspoken question: *What is this church thing my love is doing? Should I be worried?* Though this, my second marriage, was solid, I knew Bill was not likely to go with me. Bill had no church background and no inclination toward starting one now. I felt a pang for him seeing me go, and a pang for myself. I didn't want to create any distance between us. Possibly I would end this experiment in its early stages.

Although I didn't know exactly what was in store, I could reassure him today. I answered, "Uh huh, yes, I'm going to church today, but don't worry. I'm not, you know, going off the deep end." Coat in hand, as casually as possible I walked over to deliver the good-bye kiss that was, and still is, our way before parting.

Unknowingly, I was coming to the same place the much-loved author Wendell Berry had come to when he told an interviewer that he had tried to get along without church, thinking church didn't fit with being modern. Maybe, just maybe, I would find something for myself, and this something would make me happier, less hurt, less judgmental. At the very least I would learn about what I was already sure was a false dichotomy: "godless liberals" vs. "the faithful." I had seen an intriguing hint in my friend Dick Covington. He was gone now. I attended the memorial service, and like a hand-off, I would take his spot in the pews.

Spring arrived. At the beginning of Sunday service, I looked around at the assembly, strangers who week by week would turn into friends. I saw all ages in the congregation, though skewed toward the older. And styles from a few suits to Hawaiian shirts and khakis, shorts, even tank tops and slinky jersey skirts. There were more white faces than I wished at the time, with various people of color sprinkled in. That predominance of whiteness reflected the locale, with a county population at the next census still at 82% non-hispanic white. First Congregational (FCCB for short) was even a little more white than the county as a whole. On reflection, that's not necessarily a bad thing in a church. A number of Sikhs farm in northern Whatcom County, same as they do across the border in British Columbia. They have their own gurdwaras in Whatcom County. Mexicans, some of whom come to the county to work the big raspberry crop, may be more often drawn to the Catholic churches here. In any event, inclusiveness, I would soon see in FCCB, is more a matter of the heart than the arithmetic. The point isn't dilution, or assimilation to the point of erasure. And in time I would find a similar truth about other kinds of diversity at this church.

The pastor would typically open with some announcements, and then intone, "Let us worship God." The word "worship" caught at me for the piled-up meanings I'd absorbed over the years—from past churches, movies, and accounts of cults. Worship called to my mind prostrating oneself before some unseen being who presents more than a whiff of threat. Of course I also knew a comic side, like the sheet-metal thunder that the great and terrible Oz scared Dorothy with. None of that seemed to be what was meant here. Maybe the word was only being kept for tradition's sake. What new meaning I might find in "worship" was just one more question I'd need to carry in the back of my mind for a while.

I carried so many questions, each with the potential to send me packing. One basic one was from the vantage point of my sociological studies: Would church-going require an enculturation, with its own terminology, all over again, like it had in my youth? To go further with these visits might, I thought, require devoting chunks of mental space and time to getting familiar with an argot. I'd seen enough of Buddhism to know I couldn't do more there than dabble before getting into the arcane. Wasn't it going to be the same with a Christian church, if I were to get serious about joining? What would I need to understand and accept about such doctrines as the meaning of the Trinity: God, Jesus, and the Holy Spirit? Would I have to study the Bible's Old Testament again? (Stay tuned for a change in terminology.) Isn't everything that Christians need found in the New Testament, where Jesus makes his appearance and imparts his teachings? Does a progressive Christian church cherry-pick from the Old Testament in order to use its stories? Will it skirt that whole other image of God, the sometimes exasperated, jealous, even spiteful God? I felt that the Bible stories I'd grown up with were pinched at best, certainly cryptic, and often of the play-ball-with-Me-or-you'll-be-sorry variety. Bible stories also supported men's dominance over women. And the New Testament had all those letters to churches, again telling women to sit down and shut up. This church would have to have a different view of all this in order to invite me to stay.

But in contrast to my prickly questions, my Sunday experience was pleasant, even nurturing, in hymn and in sermon. I enjoyed singing old hymns, and new hymns with old melodies both beautiful and familiar. We sang of new beginnings. We sang of a spirit of gentleness. The Sunday service was earnest yet light-hearted, with plenty of room for humor. I wasn't hearing anything apocalyptic. Even so, I didn't yet dare to hope that this would turn out to be a truly different, or new, Christianity.

So I was interested to talk with my friend Jamie. She and I get together from time to time and talk over what we're each writing. The afternoon of a local Red Wheelbarrow writers get-together, before going upstairs to the banquet room for the meeting and happy hour, she and I spoke over a nice cup of soup for me and tea for her. This casual, hip dining establishment was in a relatively quiet lull. For conversation, I appreciated the absence of clinks and laughter bouncing off the high ceiling. I bent to taste my minestrone soup, then straightened up. I told Jamie I was delving into detail in a church I had started attending. She is older, like me, hikes more than I do, and goes on longer trips than I take. I admire her grit. She listened to me closely and noted that I demand more precision and understanding of the underlying context than she does. A fair and accurate observation on her part. She maybe wouldn't be surprised to learn that I sucked my thumb—as a child, of course, only as a child!—but I was an old enough child when I quit that it took the fear of discovery of my shame to make me give it up. I did show signs from an early age of trying to make my world more comforting, more long-lasting and regret-free, so that I refused myself the momentary fun of brushing a doll's coiffure because I knew the odds were against my getting it back to neat and pretty. I saw what my sister Julie's doll looked like.

I don't know if Jamie's dolls had been loved to death and messiness overlooked, but she waved a thin arm and told me, "My religious life has been reduced simply to praise and gratitude—a one-on-one between me and my Creator." She holds onto "Love God and love your neighbor." She sways to beautiful language, like "In the beginning was the Word and the Word was with God, and the Word was God." (John 1, verse one). I agreed that is beautiful and evocative. But were these words enough for my evidently ongoing need for . . . was it purity? Consistency? For actions that demonstrate that the pretty words aren't there to manipulate me? I needed underpinnings I could trust to give me some security. Maybe I even needed ongoing mothering if I could find it. A wider family to be with, certainly. Yet for Jamie, stepping out of the church was probably right. In finding the core, the beating heart, of Christianity, she's gained a way to live in this world without going to extremes. She has dug a sort of spiritual irrigation channel to nourish her garden. I wasn't quite there. Where, in nice words, even gorgeous words, was a river-worthy craft, where was fellowship?

Answers to my questions started to suggest themselves as the months went by. One Sunday, church member Anna Hall led the Time with Children. Leaning toward the children lounging on floor cushions, she concluded with, "At church we are journeying to God's heart." Together, on a journey, to God's heart. I thought that was beautiful, and maybe beauty is a way in, after all.

The sermon that followed was titled "Highest Common Denominators," launching from the Biblical passage about the griping by God's people over having only manna to eat in the wilderness after being rescued from slavery in Egypt. The sermon was by Jennifer Yokum, a tall and modest woman who, as a temporary pastor, was with us only for a short time. She asked us to see in the Hebrew scriptures—what Christians have called the Old Testament, and it is well past time to lose that term, since "Old Testament" can imply that the New Testament supersedes it—that the "thunderbolt God" can be a metaphor about the natural consequences of achieving freedom. She paused as her audience took in this idea—that there are consequences to achieving freedom. There is a lot to unpack in this one idea, and it's a topic, Jennifer said, to which Erich Fromm devoted a whole book, *Escape from Freedom*. She came to another stopper: we might want shackles because they give us an external authority to blame. When we are free, we find we miss having a ruling authority to blame. I was still mulling this as the sermon closed and the service moved on. Obviously, no one is saying it is good to be an actual slave. And American slaves who suffered horrors and death during the post-emancipation Reconstruction era, didn't seriously want to go back to slavery. But do any of us white folks escape the problem of our own freedom?

I looked up from my thoughts to find someone else was speaking from the pulpit. She was talking about a group of us going to New Orleans to help rebuild homes after the Katrina hurricane disaster. This group was called up front and we blessed them and their trip. Later we also took up a collection to support them on their way. The group made this trip annually for years and years. They found much to do in the poorer boroughs of New Orleans that U.S. society at the federal level had utterly failed to address. My friends helped save a few owners from the land sharks that swept in to profit from homeowners giving up and walking away. I was proud of these church acquaintances, and a little envious of their energy and stamina to do such a thing. The hands and feet of God in the world.

As I left that morning, it had started to rain and I was glad for the waterproof hat I'd parked on the shelf above the coats. I said my goodbyes and let my size tens take me down the wide steps, ignoring the railing that was there for safety. I looked up in an absent-minded way, gauging the rain. Big drops splashed onto my face, cool and very wet, and sent a signal to my feet to quicken my steps. My thoughts were still on Pastor Jennifer's sermon. The thunderbolt God was an apt description for the passage in the Book of Numbers, but was an image of God that had always troubled me. Jennifer had not tiptoed around it or explained it away. I was puzzled. And then it dawned on me that problematic texts, even where I might find offense, nevertheless can have their uses. Conservative Christians are not the only ones who have taken texts too narrowly, too literally. I have, too. It always sounded like a thunderous wrong, and not any kind of justice, that God would " . . .[visit] the iniquity of the fathers upon the children unto the third and fourth generation of those who hate me." (Exodus 20:5.) But ruminating, and taking this more broadly, I noticed that I don't ask Mother Nature to be fair in those terms—subsequent generations don't get to start fresh without regard for what their ancestors did to the Earth. Then the text becomes a hard but valuable lesson, rather than a narrow time-bound scripture easy to reject.

My heart was beginning to open up.

4: The Widow's Mite Story Explodes Something in Me

I listened to sermons searchingly, challengingly. I found them thought-fully put together at this Congregational church, and usually they had something brand new for me. Sometimes it was in scrutinizing a word, like "repent," which I'd associated with an emphasis on wholesale guilt and need for saving from hellfire. But it became new again when a pastor looked beyond the English to the Hebrew word and told us it means, or meant at the time, to return, to change direction. It also carries a connotation of sorrow, and had Greek precursors, with meanings of "after" and "beyond." These meanings, to me, were more human and helpful. While I'm at it, that word salvation is itself so loaded with baggage I never wanted to use it again. Fortunately, it wasn't a special attraction in the Sunday services I was attending. Maybe it adds to confusion that it gets used two ways in the Bible—physical salvation as well as spiritual. One Sunday years after, Pastor Sharon Benton unpacked the word in the course of retelling a story of healing. "Well," "whole," and "salvation" are often used interchangeably in Biblical and Hebrew texts, she said, opening her hand palm up, silently asking us if that isn't wonderful to know. It is. Knowing that helped soften my knee-jerk mind—better late than never.

By the mid-2000s, Congregationalists nationally as well as here in Bellingham were emphasizing the tagline, "God is still speaking, . . ." The comma, as opposed to a period, was a big feature of this tagline, leading to an image of God as not resting for all time on words that fit one particular era. A living God. Why, then, did so many old words, taken from old translations of the Bible, feature so often in sermons? I know, I know, this is a Christian church; what did I expect but reliance on the Bible? Yet, as I gradually learned, there is the Bible refracted through the prism of centuries of patriarchy and politics, and then there is the Bible freshly scrutinized. Often it has come as a surprise to me what our pastors have done with new interpretations. Highlighting original word meanings and the context of the times in which the texts were written changed everything for me. Biblical texts came alive, became relevant and much wiser. At coffee after the service I might remark on the sermon, or someone remark to me, and I found that others were liking what they heard, too.

Still, I squirmed when I considered calling myself Christian again. I felt that to call myself Christian would be marking myself to the wider community as old-fashioned, even a non-thinker. Nevertheless, it was clear to me I was now interested in going further than simply gaining an appreciation of the good in Christianity. I could simply be studying, like taking an art appreciation course. But I wanted to go further than a simple appreciation that would soften my past grudges, as worthwhile as that was. I loved the Biblical critiques here, and I liked these people—they impressed me as genuine, smart, even hip. I noticed they mostly didn't seem apologetic about being Christian despite the societal headwinds. Though maybe I caught a whiff here and there of hesitation to speak of it. And while I could generally find something to like about any given school of art, I surely had problems with Bible stories in general. What could this church do with those?

So I was gobsmacked to have one of my grudges get punctured and sink to the bottom, as happened next. A tired old story was the sermon's text—the widow's mites (copper coins), told in Mark 12:38-44. I hated this story, even though it was a direct teaching of Jesus, and even though it was decades gone from my mind. I groaned inwardly as the pastor, Scott Opsahl, announced from the pulpit above us what he'd be talking about. I'd heard the widow's penny, or, in the King James version, two mites, preached on at least twice before I quit church. The standard thinking matched up with *Halley's Bible Handbook* that had sat on Mom's bookshelf ever since her 1962 edition was new. Halley's was a popular authority from its first publication in 1927, and reprinted some seventy-two times. Halley says of this passage, "It was his last act in the Temple, after a day of controversy. He [Jesus] took time to pay this glowing tribute to the dear old widow who gave all she had."[1]

I can laugh now at the chip on my shoulder. I was like the deadly serious "J" in the movie "Men in Black," where he reads his alien-detecting meter and says, "We've got a bug." The smart-mouthed newbie "K" replies, "You were *stung* as a child, weren't you?" But that day I felt I'd heard all I could stand about how the widow was the exemplar of faith and self-sacrifice, this saintly woman who gave her last mites to the priest at the door. Was my distaste due only to the hackneyed exaggeration of the lesson about sacrifice? It was more than that, but I'd been taught that Halley was correct in his reading and my only choices were to be mad at the Bible or sweep this passage under the rug. What I hadn't done was to hear it read closely by a scholar on the other side of smugness.

By beginning a few verses prior to the widow's appearance in the text, Scott set up a completely different story. From verse 38 the text reads (Revised Standard Version): "And in his teaching he said, 'Beware of the scribes, who like to go about in long robes, and to have salutations in the marketplaces and the best seats in the synagogues and the places of honor at feasts, who devour widows' houses and for a pretense make long prayers. They will receive the greater condemnation.'" Ah, the temptations of privilege—don't we see it everywhere? But in Halley's gloss, this became just a "day of controversy," nothing to see here, move along, move along.

The passage continues: "Many rich people put in large sums. And a poor widow came, and put in two copper coins, which make a penny. And he called his disciples to him, and said to them, 'Truly, I say to you, this poor widow has put in more than all those who are contributing to the treasury. For they all contributed out of their abundance, but she out of her poverty has put in everything she had, her whole living.'" That's it. No actual praise for the widow.

Strange and welcome words from Scott became a new dawn. While acknowledging the common interpretation of this parable (and I loved it when pastors spoke to my thinking as if by magic—they certainly didn't know me in those early weeks), Scott said the story was really about devouring widows' houses with an implied temple admission charge. Jesus was pointing to a system that made a desperately poor woman feel compelled to give all

1. Halley, *Halley's Bible Handbook*, 479.

while others grew rich and gave proportionately little. I could recognize the familiarity of this system. I sat up straight and began to smile.

What was the basis for Jesus' rant? For that's what it was, a rant. This wasn't about just one impoverished woman. Widows are thought to have been among the poorest, most voiceless of people in the ancient societies of Jesus' time, often with no claim on property and no right to inherit. Roman law had exceptions, and there were some wealthy women. Women who owned homes even hosted the first Christian church groups. Still, it sounds like there were few merry widows in houses built by the joint contributions of the couple. Jesus wasn't praising the widow; he had other fish to fry. Rather, he was asking us all: Who benefits from this exchange? So Halley's commentary, the "glowing tribute" slant, was in my humble sociological view simply social control masquerading as Biblical authority. Dear old Dr. Halley did what comes naturally to a high-status patriarch—he interpreted the story in a way that maintains the status quo. Reinforcing the normalcy of poverty, teaching what poor women should emulate as they accept their lot. What Halley didn't say, but should have: You men of privilege, you are called upon to protect such women. Nor did Halley refer to the lesson he should have carried forward to Christian church leaders: beware of giving yourselves the honors and the good life on the backs of the poor.

All these decades of my life I have negotiated my path, and got my living, in this deeply flawed American society, and it was difficult enough on the secular side of things. Centuries removed from the day the sage and revolutionary figure of Jesus walked the dust of Galilee, it was still worth asking his questions, while so many churches bury them: Whom is being served? What is being served? The evident answers get church ditched by people like me. Now, here, in *this* church, it was obvious: the widow's mite story pointed a finger at callous injustice. This was an honest Bible story from the same old text, though inconvenient to much of institutional Christianity. I reacted as though hearing the swelling strains of the "Hallelujah Chorus." I wanted to sing.

But perversely, Handel's joyful bars suddenly gave way to Mozart's ominous chords of "Requiem." Fear rose, viscerally, almost a panic. Like a mirage, a shapeless shimmer of memory rose up, clarified, and transported me to my disastrous first marriage. Still a teen then, I tried to help a head-in-the-clouds young man. I was suddenly eighteen again, almost nineteen, in the late 1960s. I felt again the pain of the serious kid who gets to the end of childhood and finds, not answers, but a new and fraught adult world.

For me the adult world included that early marriage to a man who shut me away from my parents and friends. This new church stuff was unlocking my carefully suppressed memories of long-ago hurts.

After years living with his gradual deterioration, I escaped my first husband when he became outright dangerous. But now, so many years later, I felt the fear all over again, an irrational retrospective fear for myself. What if my early marriage had permanently derailed my college plans, the broader learning that gave me hope and pleasure and developed me into who I would become? Ten years locked in that marriage had certainly derailed my health. That long chapter in my life is something that I'd pushed so far down it was half forgotten. But it was there like a toxin, once ingested or inhaled, never to be flushed out of my tissues, but only corralled and guarded by tiny soldier cells in muscle and organ and gray matter against further injury. And here the past had arisen again, on this happy Sunday no less.

The two of us kids dropped out in 1969 after three months of a free-wheeling college scene that apparently wasn't free enough for him. My thought in following along was that he needed protection from his impracticality. But I was also lured by a kind of spiritual quest, as he was. We married for travel; in the America of 1969 we anticipated difficulty—hassle was the word then—if we were an unmarried pair. And so we went to California to find ourselves. Or transcend ourselves. It was, after all, the era of sex, drugs, and rock 'n' roll. A mash-up cultural moment of tantric yoga, Timothy Leary, and oneness with the universe. The marriage started out well enough, before his mental health slipped. Normal low-wage kids' domestic life alternated with hallucinogenic weekend experiments. Well, even our weekday domestic life wasn't actually normal. Before things got really bad, they were intermittently bad.

There was, for one instance, the kitten episode. We went to pick from a litter of kittens. The litter was classic: five or six, from a runt at one end to a dominant, aggressive kitten at the other. The rest were straight-ahead good prospects. He liked the aggressive one—thought it was the liveliest. I told him I'd grown up with cats and knew them and please, let's pick one of the middle group instead. No, it was to be his choice, and that was that. Then we got the kitten home, and he said he was going to make the cat vegetarian like we were. Naturally, I was aghast.

There existed at that time a canned soy slop, and that's what we'd feed our kitten. Oh, no, I protested, it's not in his nature. But soon there we were, our young cat becoming more and more agitated week by painful week, in a fight for its life. The frantic animal dashed about our apartment. This misery culminated in the day it got up the speed, as I can still see clearly, to circle the main room running *on the walls*. In a sit-com, that part would be funny—the story would be that the cat got into some pepper or something to excite it to that extent. But the reality wasn't funny, not for the cat, nor for me. We gave the cat away. I was glad it got a new chance at life.

Back from California, we managed to complete our bachelors' degrees, and found a job as houseparents at a halfway house in Seattle. My twenties continued, largely unplugged from the news, literature, and social contacts. And unchurched. With my harsh image of Christendom, church could be no conceivable comfort in the many trials that followed the kitten episode, nor would church get the chance to help me out of the marriage I was increasing trapped in.

Finally, ten long years in, I grabbed my own new chance at life. My leaving should have been much, much sooner. No doubt it would have been earlier with social support. Instead, it was the incipient violence in my husband's growing mental illness—for mental illness is what developed in this poor, pacifist, brilliant man—that jerked me into leaving, abruptly and with next to nothing. I couldn't help him, and staying was killing me. Reliving the misery of those years, as I was now, my neck tightened and prickly heat grabbed my back between my shoulder blades. They were years of increasing psychological abuse, in which my husband closeted me away and seemed happy only when I slumped, limp with defeat.

When I finally fled, some dear and compassionate people did stand in for a church in those early months. I called my cousin Steve, a Californian who at that time serendipitously lived in Seattle. He and his wife took me in. Steve and Kate nurtured me like a baby as I decompressed and gained strength, eating their specialty scrambled egg and green onion on mayonnaise toast. I watched Steve, handsome even in a faded old flapping shirt, bagged out pants, and overgrown curly hair, as he re-webbed the broken seats on aluminum folding chairs. Just one of the many frugal ways that allowed the couple to make it financially while buying a small old home in a run-down neighborhood. They lived a greener, smaller footprint long before the concept became popular.

I remember Steve driving me somewhere in his ancient panel truck. I forget where, but I remember the ride. I wanted to watch where we were going to learn the streets of Seattle, but I couldn't help looking down at holes and gaps in the floor under my uneasy feet. How was Steve so nonchalant when I could see the pavement zipping by inches below? I kept one eye on the bent iron gear shifter as its two-foot length wandered and waved drunkenly. Its handle was a cut glass door knob so far beyond original equipment that I laughed aloud, the first time I'd felt confident enough in my future to laugh again.

Kate also built me up with her take-no-shit straight talk about the abuse I'd been through and the right to life she encouraged me to reclaim. To my fear that my leaving would cause disaster for my soon-to-be-ex-husband—the money I'd left on the desk to make his next month's rent was all I could afford from my small salary—she said, "He's a big boy; he'll do what he needs to do." Kate, pregnant and confident, settled me down and helped put limits on the endless sense of responsibility I so often tortured myself with.

Weekdays I went to my job as the customer service representative for a tiny insurance agency. Here, too, I was met with open hearts and real help. Gordon, my boss, had a small rental house he was planning to sell but not yet, and offered it to me. Only a few blocks from the office in Seattle's Wedgwood neighborhood, it was ideal for me for a new temporary home. Gordon's partner in real estate ventures was an attorney, and he helped me navigate a divorce cheaply, spousal cooperation not forthcoming and not required. My husband had called my mother, whom he hated as a rival, thinking I must be with her, and called the office once, at first attempting to negotiate a much later divorce "after we have our student loans paid off." But somehow, perhaps with the hint of guys locking arms at the door, that was that. Things went quiet.

Still, for years afterwards I carried anxiety that he'd find me and show up on my doorstep one day after whatever self-justifying thought process might ramp up ominous intentions. This was a more realistic fear than it may sound. My own doctor told me my husband's likely condition as I described it was heritable along the male line, slow-onset, and would continue to worsen over time. The worst was the prediction that he would avoid needed medication out of a delusion that his doctors were trying to poison him. With his own father's increasingly explosive behavior as further proof for me, I'm grateful we didn't have a son.

This man I had loved was quite sincerely a pacifist. He must have strenuously worked to curb the violent impulses that his illness thrust upon him.

But he had, slowly over the ten years of our marriage, become un-hinged, while also becoming quite spoiled by my limited resistance. A col-lege friend of ours, Martha, had tried to keep in touch. When she called and said she would drop me from her annual Fourth of July party list if I stayed away yet again, I parlayed that "threat," which I half-believed, into getting my husband's acquiescence for me to go spend an hour at her party. Martha clearly was worried about me.

I had instinctively avoided saying anything that would make my husband feel afraid of me. But there came a point toward the end when I hazarded a suggestion, after I'd talked with my doctor. He'd been on another tirade about what his father might do to him. I suggested that his father might have a mental condition with a genetic basis, and that might be the threat to talk with a doctor about. A funny look came over him. He changed toward me, couldn't seem to see me anymore. Within days came the inci-dent I could not ignore: he suddenly clutched my neck in his two strong hands, his face gone mask-like. Almost nose to nose, we locked scared eyes. He sort of came to. He let go and we fell apart, both of us shocked. Clearly, he hadn't expected to act violently. Then and there in the living room of a basic apartment, our normal-married-couple facade fell away. That's when, my adrenaline still up early the next morning, I fled.

My job anchored me. My boss, Gordon, was ahead of his time, remark-able in his attitude toward the capabilities of women: women could take on any role in business, and this was as natural to his thinking as women driving cars. Gordon, my elder by more than fifteen years, gave no indica-tion that he'd evolved, as we say now; this was simply the way he had always thought. So when I got my insurance license and suggested working my way into part-ownership to allow him more time for his real estate ventures, he was willing. We went out on interesting cases, performing insurance valua-tions on businesses and fancy condo buildings and winning accounts with our knowledge and his contacts. Soon I got to hire a customer service rep to take over my old duties. A down-to-earth Catholic with an easy laugh and five children, Marilyn became a lifelong friend, the start of rebuilding a network of friends that I needed so badly.

College friends from that first freshman quarter at Fairhaven College, a small cluster college at Western Washington University, stepped in as well. It had been ten silent years, yet I was welcomed back into friendship with open arms.

When I settled down that Sunday morning from my waking night-mare and found I was still sitting safely in my usual pew a few rows back from the pulpit, my heart rate returned to normal. The heat in my back and neck subsided. I could now recognize the anger that mixed with the fear—I had pushed down anger at myself for not leaving sooner. Did my lengthy depressions in those years have a comfy side? The waste of that decade was not solely due to responsibility I felt for my ill husband. I could now see plainly it was also about avoiding responsibility to myself—responsibility to what I *could* be doing, what I could be risking (what if I failed?). Sad thoughts, but I was cleaning house; I could begin to ac-cept other factors at play. This was not just a simple psychological story of abuse and enabling. From inborn temperament to past experiences to culturally reinforced norms about masculinity and femininity, this was mostly just a part of the human story.

I felt lighter. Better for having faced a part of my past, a past that all this time could raise anxiety about a surprise knock on the door. Once back home that day my good feeling emboldened me to explore my past even further back, to look at other times of angst. I thought about my mid-teen years, when I'd had faith struggles that ultimately were part of my abandon-ing the church. The last time I had dug out my earliest journals was many years ago. Now I looked again, leafing all the way to the beginning, where the pages were unlined ecru paper, darkened over time, the pretty blue words of a fountain pen now faded, some sheets also water-spotted.

When I was fifteen, we lived in the Panama Canal Zone because of my father's work—he was a civilian accounting auditor for the Army. He took a two-year tour of duty there to get a break from Fort Lewis (Hawaii wasn't available). I joined the youth group at the local Canal Zone church. I wrote of my unsettled feelings, trying to explain them away as the restlessness of youth. "I want to conquer, see, and do, and then I'll be content to be a normal Christian adult. Plodding, quiet, caring for others, doing social work or rais-ing a family. My mind is so restless I can't even write my thoughts." And, as though continuing the same thought a year later, after we returned home to Washington State, my diary has this entry: "I can't be a Hallelujah kid, don't like mush, but I need the spirit of God. Is a puzzlement. But it's also stupid to spend your whole life puzzling out an identity, truth, and all the other bunk." As a reminder, this is a sixteen-year-old's diary; well, at this point, I was seventeen. It continues: "I'm torn between the traditional Christian ide-als about marriage, birth, work, and death (I can't reject them), and modern, at least radical but not unreasonable thoughts on these things." Even then I was gradually rejecting the Christianity I knew.

In Panama, my parents certainly didn't spout religion, though Mom and her girls attended the Canal Zone church in our small community of Curundu. The church was a supposedly inclusive, generic Christian church of no discernible denomination, but it bore earmarks of American Restoration Movement churches I later learned about. They tried to return to the purposes of the first-century churches and find unity getting away from creeds that divided denominations in Protestantism. A noble instinct, to be sure. However, they held that the New Testament, and its then-current English translation, was perfect, unerring, etched in stone. Perhaps these Restoration churches are only subtly different from other conservative theological stances—they seem to believe that, as Rob Bell says, "there is an ideal state or culture or way of doing things that if you could just get back there, then you'd be all set."[2] In contrast, Bell bids us learn to see to see the movement, the story arcs, in the Bible. My new church in this new century was now taking me in that new direction, and church was showing me the logic, and the excitement, of "God is still speaking."

In Panama, I was baptized full immersion, which was one of the American Restoration beliefs, that full immersion was necessary for salvation. I came up and dripped my way back onto the sandy shore and the waiting towel handed to me by my sister Julie. I remember feeling embarrassed by this salvation thing. I didn't plan to discuss it with Dad—I'm sure he would only have said something noncommittal, but I didn't want to go there. The ceremony of baptism can be lovely whether immersion or a sprinkle, but not if the words spoken and the church family are wrong for you.

Early the next year, as I approached eighteen, my journal showed the last gasps of my religious struggle. "One thing I think about is that Christianity doesn't seem to fit the whole world." Which wouldn't have mattered if you weren't so hard-shell literal about THE way, THE truth, and THE life. Too bad I didn't know there were important differences among Christian churches. By the time I left home for college, I had exciting new areas of study to think about. I had quit the religious arena.

I had no worry now, in this church in Bellingham, about faith struggles. No straitjackets to push against when I had a question or concern. I was free to paddle according to what the waters presented. And a key for me was how thoroughly I was shown that these Congregationalists are

2. Bell, *What Is the Bible*, 131

quite comfortable that a woman's place in the church is everywhere, leading as often as not. That's both in laity leadership—the church moderator, for instance, is a woman as often as a man—and in preaching. Pastor Jane Sorenson is a case in point, standing before us with the colorful stole marking ordination hanging to below her knees. So comfortable with her role, she let her delicious sense of humor shine amid her serious messages. Equality of women was not a trumpeted thing, just a bit more proof seen each Sunday. Gay and lesbian members were likewise elevated to leadership roles at First Congregational Church of Bellingham, even in my earliest visits in the mid-aughts. The church has been the better for diverse contributions.

Satisfied for now with this particular church's modern attitudes toward women, I was willing to set aside, at least for a time, my problem with Christian traditions about Easter, and with some New Testament passages, keeping a separate mental cupboard to shut away the exhortations attributed to Paul that sound so anti-equality today. Much the same way as my mother must have done with texts that felt wrong. Mom didn't say anything to me. But in watching her, I got clues as to how she could live with conservative Christian teachings. The tips she had for me about being a woman in our broader society were similar to how I saw her behave within church: walk with strength and purpose when you are alone, get assertive but only from time to time, and build circles of women friends.

Mom might have feared going against teachings, but she acted as though God is bigger than some of the things she learned in Bible study groups. Now it was my turn in life, and my choice. I couldn't just forget my concerns about Christian teachings, nor keep them locked away for long if I were to continue with this attempt to be in church again. I was going to unpack them one by one.

Much later, while writing this memoir, I saw plenty of evidence that my new church hadn't just willed equality into Christianity, but it was already there, even if you had to dig. Surprisingly, there was a woman apostle, an apostle who preached and taught and who was praised by none other than the apostle Paul. Then a purposeful falsehood was inflicted in the twelfth century on the text in Romans 16:7 that refers to her. According to scholar Rena Pederson, who gathered together the evidence that most scholars agree on now, religious authorities changed "Junia" to a male-sounding name, Junias, a made-up name not appearing in any of the other literature of the day. Poof! She's gone, the fact of her femaleness well-buried, allowing Paul's acknowledgment of her status as one of the few apostles to be buried as well and the apostles to morph into an all-male club. The King James version had her name right. Scholars have now restored her name in the New Revised Standard Version of the Bible and some other versions. But even where the text is accurate, the brevity of the reference to Junia is still easily overlooked.

Actually, out and out perfidy didn't have to be involved. The men working over the texts centuries later would have found the idea of a woman in an exalted role inconceivable. And so they may have thought they were simply correcting the text.

Deep, fearless reading of scripture is a type of conservatism long overdue. Now I could begin to see the depths of the river and not only the cold glitter of its surface.

5: Who Are These People?

Often we were singing hymns new to me. One that became a favorite was written in 1978, during the time I never entered a church anywhere and didn't know what was going on beneath the mass media's reportage about Christian churches. Titled "Spirit, Spirit of Gentleness," the note at the bottom of the hymnal page says it was first sung at Waiokeola Congregational in Honolulu, and a church member there offered a suggestion, which author James K. Manley ran with, adding a fourth stanza. A contribution from the pews sounds exactly like the Congregational way, and very like the poets among us now. That fourth stanza about women and men seeing clearly and making new decisions speaks to my lifelong disagreement with some currents in American culture and the stories we tell ourselves. I'm thinking of the currents that still tie wealth to virtue, and poverty to laziness, that value men over women, and condone cruelty toward immigrants, or turn a deaf ear to the ideas of younger generations.

In the community church I attended in the Panama Canal Zone, "Spirit, Spirit of Gentleness" would not have been their type of hymn. This newer hymn does, however, fit with FCCB's radical welcome and their early stand for same-sex marriage. It fits with resistance to poverty and plunder—resistance to being complacent, to me a vital resistance. I was noticing that many in this church give substantial sums to charitable groups. Not something individuals speak about, but it's in the reports of church endowments, scholarships, and in totals collected for special mission offerings. Maybe that giving spirit was where the missing jewelry "went," the jewelry I hadn't seen on my first visit to this church, when I saw well-dressed people but not bling. The words we sang about bold new decisions inflamed my hopes of doing something together about the degradation of our Earth. And increasingly, about our democracy itself. Even if I didn't know all the members, I knew this congregation was different from any I'd seen.

So who are these people who come faithfully to this church on Sundays and whose cars and bicycles populate the parking lot on weekdays as well? I wanted to know where all this came from. When I was a child, the United Church of Christ (UCC) was in its infancy, grafted together in 1957 from very old branches that were then ready to consolidate. That is how FCCB got its awkward slashed name: First Congregational Church of Bellingham/ United Church of Christ. FCCB joined the new UCC immediately. With a motto: "That we may all be one. In essentials, unity. In non-essentials, diversity. In all things, charity."

Absent are tests of faith. The mind, the word, are the emphasized avenue toward God, but importantly, seeing the word as not locked in the Bible, but springing forth from it; that if we listen, God is still speaking. Despite the overall declining trend in church-going, the UCC comprises 4,800 churches in the U.S. This is a major current in the river but it's not splashy—it doesn't grab headlines. I am chagrinned that I thought progressive churches were invisible.

In fact, I had a welcome early memory of church in childhood, in a Congregational church in Seattle. It was a rare liberal church experience in my past, though as a child I wasn't aware what the difference was. In the family's two years in Seattle in the late 1950s, my father, to all appearances an unbeliever, steered us to University Congregational Church, where we all, parents and kids alike, revered its pastor, Dr. Dale Turner. My father's motivation may have been to gain cachet at his office or bridge club, since there were respected, prosperous people at this church. No doubt this choice of church also served to achieve a compromise with my mother, who wanted the whole family to attend church if possible, though she leaned toward a more familiar down-home branch of Christianity.

Dale Turner, with the kid-friendly homilies he gave before we trooped off to Sunday school, was a spellbinder for all of us. I didn't recall him ever talking hellfire in that 1959 oasis of Seattle liberalism, but after attending conservative churches, I'd thought maybe it was out of some kind of politeness, that possibly his Congregational church believed the same things as the churches we called fundamentalist. Because there is just essentially one Protestant Christianity, right? Then we moved to Tacoma, and Mom and her girls went to Baptist, then Methodist, churches, which I didn't like nearly as well, though I tried to. Dad stayed home on Sundays.

The people I was meeting at FCCB seemed well-grounded. Like they were part of something with sturdy roots. So I was intrigued to delve into the lineage of this place. Our church was formed in 1883 when Pastor Joseph Wolfe came here to establish a church in a rough-cob settlement of lumber workers and fishers. Pastor Wolfe and some volunteers dragged lumber up from the mill on the bay to the first site at F Street and Astor. The church bell arrived as a gift in 1884, traveling by ship all the way around the Horn from New York. Members lent their muscle to get the heavy bell up the muddy hill from the bay. Once in place in the bell tower, the bell also served the larger community, calling firefighters and, during the Depression of 1893–97, ringing when soup was ready to share. This history helped me understand how much sheer work it is to make and keep a church.

Some hard times followed for the little church. In the stock market crash of 1893, the successor pastor couldn't be paid, so he left, ushering in a seven-year period when four pastors came and went. In 1901, the church sold subscriptions for a new church building on H Street. That building wasn't finished to modern standards, however—it had only a dirt floor basement with dampness problems, and rats nested in the organ pipes. The church membership grew for a while, then declined in the years 1908–1915. Still they paid off the debt. There was also a year when frozen pipes created a horrifying plumbing bill, and the time during WWI, when they had no pastor, and the organist had to buy the choir music out of her $25 monthly salary. The infamous flu epidemic of 1918–19 cancelled services for three or four months. In the 1920s, H Street, where the church sat, lay unpaved. The sidewalks were failing and streetcar service was lost, even as Sunday school outgrew its space and curtain partitions had to be put up in the Sanctuary for classes. In the inauspicious year of 1929, the church purchased property at the present site, D Street and Cornwall. Fund-raising went on through the Great Depression. Finances became desperate by 1932, yet they finally broke ground in June of 1937 and completed the building the next year.[1]

1. Murray, *Centennial Churches*, 53–68.

The FCCB building didn't reach its current size until 2003, with a new Sanctuary seating 350, the old Sanctuary becoming the social hall. The approval of the capital campaign came in 1999, the same momentous year as the vote to become Open and Affirming, which formally welcomed gay, lesbian, and transgender people. Some of today's old members worked on this huge building expansion project, such as Carole G, who remains a head usher, bustling about and never dropping a stitch. Permit me a private grin, because I also know her antic side. The building costs were held down with the help of 6,000 volunteer hours like hers. That is a lot of heavy lifting before I ever got there.

6: Joining Up

At this time that I was getting to know First Congregational, I had been a Big Sister through Big Brothers/Big Sisters for two or three years, starting when my Little—I'll call her Celie—was about eleven. When we were introduced she was playful and bright, if reticent about herself, while nevertheless observing me closely. I was the same age as her grandmother, but they matched us due to some common interests and however else they do their wizardry. Celie's parents were divorced; she lived with two younger brothers and her mother. I felt that Celie's mother was a good parent doing her best for her children, and had applied to Big Brothers/Big Sisters as another resource.

From the beginning, it was up to me how to offer a friendship that Celie would accept and reciprocate—that she would feel any confidences were safe—a relationship we could take into her teens. Somehow we got there, starting with snacks and play. Frisbee was new to her and she couldn't seem to get the hang of the wrist action. I felt my age when bending again and again to retrieve errant tosses. We moved on to my kitchen. She put on the apron I had cut down to her size, and I asked her to whisk something, only to reveal the same wrist frustration. After some practice didn't unlock this skill, we worked around it. But improv! Celie had a dynamite facility for verbal creativity. I especially remember the laughs we had by adorning our talk with "dude," which was having a pop culture moment then. First a sprinkling, then one day as I kept both hands on the steering wheel and we used no gestures but only our voices, we had an entire conversation consisting only of the one word, inflected into two, even three syllables. We flew like Frisbees.

We hopped boulders at the saltwater shore of Boulevard Park, traded music choices in the car and at home, where we could dance and get silly. This was all great, for me as well. However, it came time for our friendship to be more than an escape from conflict at home. Celie was getting emotionally closed-in as living arrangements changed—she went to live with her father for a while in a nearby town, and later back to Bellingham with her grand-mother—and these moves shuffled her from one school to another.

She revealed some fears to me. Including, hard for me to imagine, of tap water. And of horses, and this pinged my heart, having been comforted often by my love of horses—I had figurines and books, and occasionally rode when I was her age.

It happened that the daughter of church acquaintances, the Ken-nells, had an unusual therapy practice in which her horses took center stage, and they suggested I call Ginger. I quickly did call, looking not for a course of therapy, which was not my place to arrange, but just a meet-and-greet with her horses. Ginger assured me that it would be just the thing to bring Celie out for a visit, and she'd be glad to show us her magic. Ginger's practice builds on the wisdom of the original horse whisperer, Monty Roberts, and his discoveries about equine communication. You don't want to subdue a horse; you want to get the horse to join with you. Having studied the similarities between horses and people, Ginger helps young people with problems that tend to isolate them. She helps them to experience the beauty of "joining up."

Some distance out into farming territory, we found Ginger's address. Celie and I turned into the driveway that ran alongside the old house and stopped at a weathered outbuilding. Celie had been quiet on the drive, and I worried a little at how stiffly she sat clutching her pink music player. But now we were here. I saw her look at the fences and barn—safe bar-riers!—and she seemed to relax a bit. Then Ginger came striding toward us with the right mix of interest, softness and confidence, and Celie put herself in Ginger's hands.

That afternoon, while I waited at the far corner of the grey-weathered fence, Celie met animals who by nature have conflicting tendencies—to flee or to investigate. Ginger selected Cheveyo, as she often did for fearful clients. Celie learned to read Cheveyo's body language and to become aware of her own. In only an hour, after exercises in moving away and moving closer, Celie was smiling and clearly comfortable standing near and facing the gentle Cheveyo, who had accepted her and was willing to, so to speak, join her herd. As Celie stroked his black-brown neck, I wondered if she was enjoying the grassy scent of horses I had always liked. From the railing of the corral I saw her titter as the horse's snuffling warm breath and big, loose lips brushed her skin, and I wanted to sing. The song that came to me was the oldie, "Someone's in the Kitchen with Dinah," and I hummed *Someone's in the paddock with Chev-o, Someone's in the paddock I know - o - o -oh.* Banjo, fiddle, and frog! I tapped a cordovan demi-booted toe against hard dirt, because that's what you have to do when the cowbell sounds. No barriers for Celie. No fears. All friends. *Dude.*

My own skittish flee-or-investigate approach to this church had settled into comfortable familiarity. My visits had proven stimulating, affirming, and sociably sweet. I could see I was not going to be asked to profess or even believe the tenets built up like barnacles over the centuries. I didn't have to believe that Jesus' death was a planned sacrifice for sin. I didn't even have to believe God is a patriarch—this church calls God "Creator," or "Mother and Father God." Church now looked like a life's work consisting of following and practicing. Rather than a transaction of being saved, so called, I would be following Jesus, who to all evidence I could find was pro-women's equality. Those were reasons enough to join, even if I wasn't always at home with the litany if it turned to the old, unexamined version I once knew. On the whole, this church was right for me. Really, that meant: good for me. And this church wasn't only about feeding and guiding the intellect. The support and acceptance needed even by middle-class people was palpable here, and emotionally authentic. I got no sense anyone was simply going through the motions. What kind of church has an office manager who closes her emails with a Dietrich Bonhoeffer quote about driving a spoke into the wheel of injustice? I liked that spirit.

At home, our Sunday pancake breakfasts resumed—when we could get up early enough. Bill and I didn't really talk about the step I contemplated of joining the church; maybe it was just a gradually arriving thing that was understood. Or we handled it obliquely, as we do many things. With humor. We're movie buffs, and the day after viewing a favorite comedy, "Cactus Flower," I left Bill in front of the TV where football blared, saying to him as Ingrid Bergman said to Walter Matthau, "Fine. You go to your church and I'll go to mine." Bill chuckled. An old expression with a lot of wisdom in it.

Part of the Sunday pattern is the offering. Various members volunteer to give a short personal reflection before asking the ushers to come forward and collect the offering. The gratitude individuals express for the church can floor me. One came from Bert M., a gay woman I already knew and liked, but as she told her story, a story of ridicule at school and sorrow growing up, followed by being frozen out at other churches, she started to tear up. Her story cemented my solidarity with her, and added to my perspective on this church. You don't have to be poor to be hurting, and it was welcoming to me personally to hear this acknowledged. She and her wife continue to be role models for what it is to be kind and loving Christians—I know her kindness from the way she checks in on me and from her active support and friendship for others—Bert has a special quality that infuses her voice and unadorned face with beauty.

I learned a new hymn, "Draw the Circle Wide," by Gordon Light and Mark Miller. More anthem than typical hymn, it was a rouser whose title I'd spotted in the hymnal on my first visit. The words lean hard on images of solidarity. We stood in our pews—side by side, of course, as in the hymn—and the chorus declared that no one stands alone. It felt so good. I had found a church home. Here I might even be able to fully reclaim Christianity for myself—church and Christianity not necessarily being one and the same. To echo the Seattle poet Elias Cotez, who once commented about a different scene, the underground music and culture scene in Seattle, remarking how good it felt to be there pursuing things that would be lasting.

I'd had a dim view of hard-shell Christians with their complacent certainty. And I've been dismayed by what I'll call hard-shell atheists, not only for the certainty of their pronouncements (and assumptions) but their disdain for anyone who didn't subscribe to their brand of thinking. Now I was confronting my own conceptions of the church, the edges of my own shell of objection had softened. Here I could plant myself and grow. Surely now that I was no longer at my job where I'd been nudged and inspired by my manager and co-workers, I needed a group to join. If I didn't have an important membership central to my life, I felt I would sag into . . . exactly what, I wasn't sure. But I needed to belong somewhere, and this seemed a not-bad fit. Not bad at all. So in the spring of 2005, while the rhodies bloomed, and we had pressure-washed the winter's accumulation of algae off the back deck, on Sundays I went to the inquirers' class for prospective new members.

Finding the Fireplace Room the first time, I emerged out of the plain broad hallways into an inviting, if bigger than average, living-room. Homey wood-paned windows let the outdoors in on three sides. It was a sunny morning. I took in the lightly patterned blue and grey couches, rockers, and square coffee table, and chose a seat from among easy chairs. Two couples were there for the same purpose, both somewhat older than I, and one other woman. We learned church history, the role of doctrine, how we work through the life of Jesus and birth of the church in the church year. Our year progresses from autumn's Advent season and Christmas, to Epiphany in the New Year, on through Jesus' ministry to Lent, then Easter and Pentecost—known as the birth of the church—to "ordinary time" and finally to Advent again. As to topics, we have a three-year cycle. That was good to know, because I intended to attend regularly and didn't want twelve months to exhaust interesting topics.

Scott Opsahl was the pastor at this time, an interim pastor but serving quite a while. His manner was what I imagined a silver-haired seminary professor would be like, if that professor was approachable. I enjoyed the questions and enthusiasm of the others, and I sat comfortably and listened intently as Scott told us how participation in Christianity had split up into different emphases—different styles. Where the Bible speaks of using your heart, mind, and soul and strength, different denominations each claimed one emphasis as its leading style. Heart—the Biblical seat of one's will—became the banner of Baptists (*make* that decision). Strength, or body, was emphasized by Catholics and the Christian Orthodox, with prominent roles for incense, kneeling, beads, statues. Soul, the deepest part of us, that we are emotional about, became the focus of Pentecostals. And Mind, using your mind in the service of God, became the emphasis of Congregationalists. That explained the thoughtful sermons, the ease around changing one's mind, not suppressing one's thoughts, which was what drew me in.

More recently, churches have been responding to an urge to put it all back together again. FCCB's worship services are re-integrating all four avenues for loving God—more participation, more visuals, restoring ancient practices like walking a labyrinth, meditative pauses, loosening our bodies in response to music. More food, more candles, and artful, fluttering banners. And always continuing a big emphasis on community. Newer architectural ideas, more in the round like our Sanctuary, supported interaction.

Church was where we could get different eyes. An imaginative vision, as if we could see from God's eyes, and feel touched and seen as well.

I once took as mildly sacrilegious a track of the famous album, "Tommy," by The Who. The worshipful "See Me, Feel Me" sings of someone charismatic and Jesus-like. Now I find that the song enters me deeply. It's an aching, insistent rock anthem—about feeling the touch, the healing, the heat, and finding the glory, a glory that isn't about painted haloes but rather a radiant spiritual experience bubbling up through me. I didn't know how much I craved that emotional flow. Of course, for me, emotions were not yet, and maybe never will be, a smooth free-flow. It's as though a cruelly tight corset from the past has found me, wrapped itself around my middle, and has me looking for the fainting couch of old. My emotions tend to bang around in my chest and leave me fatigued and not breathing comfortably. Too many years of holding emotions at bay. But if even just a part of the energy can make it down to my feet, I dance it out and I'm younger than young for a while, alive and fully awake.

As I sat with the other prospective members, my thoughts eagerly leapt to: What will we engage with next? Thinking "We." I felt I'd found my tribe. I didn't yet know how I was going to get along with the Bible, with scriptures that give me heartburn, or with terms like "worship," or for that matter with prayer. My quest into a faith to fully love would have to continue. But I found I was happy to be here. So, with hope that I could again call myself, and become, a Christian, I joined. I stood in front of the congregation and made my avowals, and the congregation in response made their promises to me and the others that day: a warm welcome to a community, "not of the sinless, but of fellow seekers of new ways of being in relationship with God and enacting God's intention for the wholeness of humankind." I didn't believe God was literally an intentional sort of being, but this church itself felt like it had a group intention for wholeness. I trusted I would find my zone.

You might say I liked my new canoe even though the trim wasn't yet tuned for me. Trim is the term for the seating adjustments—forward or backward—that bring the bow and stern into a weight balance. When the trim wasn't good, Bill being quite a bit heavier, I rode high in the bow, almost out of the water, till we slid and locked the seats for a nice level water line. In church my baggage in the stern still weighed it down. My canoe floated, but it might want to go in circles, or take on water, until the trim resolved.

If a church doesn't q-u-i-t-e fit, maybe it's the trim. And you can do something about that.

7: First Duties

My first roll-up-sleeves involvement was with the Diaconate Board. Nice folks, all ten or so of them, most of them women. Boards are like standing committees. The Diaconate's purview is to recruit ushers and greeters, help officiate at Communion, and help the pastors with planning the Sunday worship service. Since I was still uncomfortable with the term worship, I'm pretty sure I ended up on this board by being asked rather than volunteering. Pastor Scott held a retreat and over refreshments explained the ecclesiastical (churchy) reasons for the order of Sunday worship—why the various aspects (the call to worship, prayers and hymns, children's message, scripture reading, sermon, offering, benediction) were ordered as they were. I learned a lot, though some of the more arcane reasons for the particular order of worship left my memory quickly; common sense seemed just as good an explanation. I was surprised that a prayer of confession is in every Sunday service. Put that way, it sounds so like a Catholic ritual. But on Sundays at FCCB it is never the same prayer; it is engagingly new each Sunday. The prayer of confession is always related to the sermon that will follow. I grew to appreciate the many varied and creative prayers we say together, such as one confessing that naming our brokenness aloud is not comfortable, yet we trust God and those around us to have compassion. And one that nudged us to confess that we often choose comfort over change. This prayer also allowed us to confess that we sometimes keep silent when others need us to speak, and we sometimes speak when others need us to hear their voices. Such prayers balance the age-old dual roles of the church: to comfort, yes, and also to challenge.

I did not, by the way, *ask* in Diaconate training about a key foundational word like worship. I was afraid it would expose me, label me somehow. I guess my trust was not complete, and my vulnerability to embarrassment also held me back. I preferred to observe, and turn things over in my mind on my own.

It occurs to me that this working things out privately is a lifelong trait: Mom told me about my first spoken word. No undignified gurgles nor even momma/dadda preceded the forming of a perfect word. I was upstairs in my crib supposed to be asleep. Evidently I could hear my parents downstairs at a card table with friends, and Mom, whose voice carried well, several times said my father's name, Ed. Maybe she said it firmly, signaling that she didn't like his bid. They all had a laugh when they heard me bellow an extended "Ed! . . . Ed!" Mom and Dad trotted up to congratulate me, and found me on my feet, grasping the crib's top rail, still repeating what I proudly knew to be correct.

In this case, I tucked the word worship away in that cupboard of mine and enjoyed helping in the various parts of the service. I must not have been the only one bothered about the word worship, because it came up in a sermon. The pastor, perhaps it was Jane, told us worship was about where we put our hearts—with reverence, devotion, and thanksgiving. This meaning I liked, though I wanted more to hang it on. Later I was happy to know it's a perfectly good word I needn't be afraid of. A church member passed along an essay by a New Zealand Christian theologian, Lloyd Geering, who said that "the etymology of the word is 'worth-ship'. . . We participate in a ceremony or drama which expresses what we deem to be of great worth to us."[1] Finally, a scholarly approach. This was more than cool with me. Then I thought, how many *secular* words have connotation baggage—even bad memories—for you or me? We have to allow church words the same forbearance, really, otherwise we'd continually have to invent new words. I appreciate that church words don't change as fast as does slang. It's better that way.

Autumn came with the sweet season of brilliant color, dotting the town and drenching our home garden, which thanks to Bill has not only

1. Geering, "Venerable New Church," 23.

rhododendrons and native cedars, firs and big-leaf maples, but tree selections of his. Like a stewartia (Japanese stewartia pseudocamellia) that I had planted in the rain (and mud) one day with a community college student named Colin while Bill had to rest his back. Our stewartia was now spreading a rosy-orange glow in a bed we built around it. Our Japanese maples bathed the eye in colors from lacy scarlets to buttery yellows, or tricolor like the grape-leaf maple growing bigger each year on the east side of our place, the leaves hemmed in green and yellow, with a cantaloupe-orange slip showing. We hadn't minded the work of building the low crescent of a stone wall below the tree to reduce the slope and keep this magnificent tree from drying out in the summer. And didn't mind the raking that followed the flagrant beauty. Well, we did start hiring university students to help.

Then at the end of December, our family got the hard news that my sister Rosemary's cancer had returned, after nearly five years. I didn't share much about my sister's illness with church acquaintances, partly because of another discomfort I had. I was balled up over any prayer not ritualized with a script. Private prayer, the concept and the practice, was shut away in my cupboard. If others knew of Rosemary's illness, they'd offer to pray for us, and private prayer to me still meant, erroneously, the kind we prayed in the church of my teens, in Panama, where you ask God as depicted by Michelangelo on the Sistine ceiling to reach out his finger to change something in your favor. But this concern to avoid being a fraud by solemnly accepting prayers did keep me a bit apart during a time I could have used support. I could have expressed my discomfort with my previous experience with prayer and these good folks would have taken it in stride. But I didn't know that then. I just let my shoulders hunch a bit and carried on.

For that matter, and even more important at that time, I couldn't expose myself to attention on my emotions. I was barely keeping myself together, and didn't want *inquiry* for goodness' sake. This was my loss, I know, but that's where I was. Expressions of support would raise emotion, and getting emotional always seemed to come with a cost: a hurting in my diaphragm that could affect my breathing for days. That corset again. That was a frailty amid my overall good health that left me quite sure I was weird. But no, it was more likely that I hadn't quenched my habit of suppressing strong emotion—often suppressing it right where I breathe. I say habit as though it was something I just fell into. But I didn't just *happen* to develop a habit of holding my breath. And it went further back than my walking-on-eggshells first marriage. A family dynamic plays into it, as I would come to understand, but not yet.

My heart's opening to prayer crept up on me like a lullaby. I noticed the effect on me of part-time pastor Deanna's voice in prayer, a voice so gentle and calm that it could tame the emotional dragons I'd closed myself off to avoid. Even the smallest children seemed to quiet themselves when Deanna spoke. Prayer in this church, by the pastors anyway, was for comfort and presence, not miracles. I took my issue with private prayer out of the cupboard from time to time and looked at it gently. Prayer doesn't have to mean supplication. Prayer has similarities to meditation in that it frees my mind from hurry, and from conventional thinking that tethers me to the visible surface of things. Eventually I came to like it. Prayer tilts me toward others more than does meditating on my own mind. Prayer, maybe on a walk and not in a classically prayerful pose, lets me go deep into a place of oneness with someone whose situation is on my mind. It lets this deep place create my response.

My attendance at church grew spotty as I made the two-hour trips to Tacoma starting in late 2005—there was plenty to do with and for Rosemary and her husband and daughter in that sad and stressful time. I was grateful that my relationship with Rosemary could grow closer. She and I had often been at odds as adults, as conservatives and liberals can be. It's funny that she had been the one who sneaked out of the house at night to go smoking with other delinquents, while I was the upright oldest sister.

Rosemary and I did have areas of agreement, like about Dad and about Mom. And often we had the same ideas about what was fun, and funny. Before she got sick the second time, Rosemary and I traveled together to see Dad in the Phoenix area. We had just arrived at the home of Lynette and Ron, close friends of hers who had invited us to stay with them for the week, when, getting out of our rental car, Rosemary's thin jeans burst open at the seat. The rip was so bad the pants would hardly hold together. As Lynette came out to greet us she found us helpless, bent over and snorting with laughter that went on and on before we could even say Hi. That episode of hilarity cleared the cobwebs between us sisters like nothing else.

When Rosemary was fighting cancer and I was with her more, we had time that I'm endlessly thankful for—talking about family, visualizing ourselves as sea grasses in the waves, watching cooking shows, and getting to doctor appointments. Rosemary died mid-2006.

Soon after, while still deflated by Rosemary's death, I helped Mom move up to Bellingham, and my daily life re-patterned itself. Rosemary had warned that Mom angles to be joined at the hip with the nearest daughter. I didn't doubt it. I knew that Mom, while on extended stays with Rosemary and family, had even gone through their garbage for things that were "still good." I was a bit sympathetic to Mom about this, but you have to respect the householders. When her new life at The Willows Senior Apartments began to eat up my energies—though I enjoyed having Mom close by—I was soothed by sermons like Jennifer Yokum's that August from a text in Ephesians. The Biblical metaphor was about putting on the suit of armor of God, and Jennifer made the point that metaphors are all we really have, and how they point to, but are not themselves, truth with a capital T. Jennifer liked to adopt a metaphor different from the traditional one of the soldier. She liked to think of the suit of the cook: rubber clogs so as not to slip, an apron of hospitality, an oven mitt to handle the heat, the hat of wisdom, and of course the spoon of generosity. The feminine tilt to this metaphor delighted me, especially since I was cooking more and more from scratch. The metaphor, carried further, points to the idea of feeding, rather than fighting, one's enemy. I wondered how that could work. But it was delight-fully chewy. And fragrant like the rich smell in my kitchen of Moroccan spices that I was experimenting with.

Those were merely stray musings as I found myself busy with family. In addition to doing for Mom and going on outings with Mom, soon I also needed to take a more active role with my aged father in Arizona (Mom and Dad had divorced decades ago). There were phone calls, long-distance handling of his requirements, and week-long trips. Dad died in 2010. So for those years of double coverage—care for parents who were a thousand miles apart, I didn't participate much at church outside of attending Sunday services.

One touchstone for me was, unexpectedly, Communion. FCCB offers this sacrament on the first Sunday of each month. It is a simple rite: first a spoken reminder of Jesus' Last Supper behest—do this in remembrance of me—then blessing the elements, then everyone, members and non-members who wished to participate, one pew at a time, sliding out to the aisle on their left, coming forward, receiving a torn piece of whole wheat bread (or a gluten-free cracker), dipping it into sweet purple grape juice from a proffered glazed earthenware chalice, hearing murmured words of blessing from the pastor or Diaconate member holding the chalice, and moving off to the right to return to their pew. How was it that such ordinary elements added up to an always-moving sacrament? A big part of it was just that we were together, in this time and place, and experiencing this spirit of peace together, whether we met others' eyes or just saw others looking inward, cupping their dipped bread with a hand to catch any drip, maybe carrying it to their pew to take when they were ready. It felt, and still feels, like we are blessing one another, not just receiving a blessing from a highly trained official, though that is powerful, too. I love this mystery each time.

As I got to know the various families, I saw how often family groups sat scattered in the Sanctuary. They couldn't sit together if Nancy sang in the choir, and her husband David didn't. Or teenager Emma needed to sit in the right-hand section behind the pastors to be ready to hop up several times to read the liturgy, her parents remaining in their favorite spot near center front. There are many parts to be played on a typical Sunday. Even more on those Sundays when the bell choir, in their white gloves, rings out a tune, or Advent candles are lit by a dad and child. The first meaning I pull from the broad participation is that the old days of rolling up sleeves to keep the church going weren't the exception but the rule. The more exciting thing I noticed was how this helped make real what we say about our church family. Participants weren't really separated from their families in seating—instead they sat with members of their wider family. This differs from the image of church services in the movies, where nuclear families are together and all are in the audience, not leaving their pew.

This "we're family" approach is not the same as the sociological notion of the church as family surrogate, at least as analyzed in a 1960s academic book, *To Comfort and to Challenge: A dilemma of the Contemporary Church,* by Glock et al. Retired Episcopal priest and friend Armand Larive offered it to me for my background research. I was glad to recognize one of the authors as a major name in sociology, though I didn't need to worry—Armand is no slouch—he wouldn't have junk literature in his library. These sociologists at mid-century examined how they found churches functioning for their members, and a leading idea was that especially for the singles, church members were in effect surrogate family. My membership felt like considerably more than that to me, and of course I already had a family. Even if Bill and I were without children, we had siblings and nieces and nephews. No doubt church can be a family surrogate for some, a filling of a lack. But there's a different vibe here. For instance, one woman leads some of the music from her battery-powered chair, thereby serving rather than being served. And those whose spouses don't often attend for whatever reason, plug themselves into whatever they enjoy, whether it's the choir or the coffee service or a special non-Sunday interest circle like the knitters. The folks I'm thinking of don't lack families; church simply lets them step into a bigger, wider group that nevertheless feels like family.

I liked being in this church family. About Christianity I continued to hold something back and keep my own counsel, even as I enjoyed singing and being together. After my discomfort on Palm Sundays two years in a row, I thought I'd have to skip the crucifixion story permanently when it came around every Easter. This was because Easter time sometimes came with old-style prayers and scripture flatly repeating that God had sent his Son to die for us. And I just couldn't feel that this fit a modern church, and certainly didn't fit my own spiritual needs. What I wanted was the prophet and rabbi Jesus, who was a brave, profound, and God-filled teacher, who asked others into a way of life. I couldn't see how it helped me follow Jesus to make the end of his life a human sacrifice story, especially framed as a sacrifice for us, required by God. Which, to be sure, went a giant step beyond what this church of mine actually espoused. Even with this church not taking that step, I still clenched. That is, if the story meanings were as I thought, and that was a big if. I assumed I knew the meanings, and had reason to reject them. I'd have to set this all aside for awhile, and I did. Like a hot poker. And so I found my spirit fed in singing "You Have Come Down to the Lakeshore." In Spanish. The melody is known all over the world—it's the Spanish "Pescador de Hombres" by Cesáreo Gabaraín. It's beautiful, very Spanish in flavor. I am humming it as I write and wish I could share the sound of it.

We were still in a lengthy period of temporary pastors. In joining when I did, I had missed the long tenure of a beloved lead pastor, and what he brought of, well, security I imagine it was. Then when we finally thought we had a new lead pastor, he became ill and died within months of beginning with us, leading to more grief, and more temporaries, who concentrated on keeping the flock together during a time of wandering and waiting. We had rules against hiring a temporary pastor as permanent. The rules have good reasons, and indeed, the typical temp is not looking for a permanent position, but we said good-bye to several I liked a lot—Scott Opsahl for one, and another, Jane Sorenson, terrific and well-loved, as I've said, for her marvelous sense of humor.

The changing pastors complicated any evolution of mutual theological understandings between pastor and congregation, not to mention complicating any big new social or environmental justice initiatives that might arise. This disappointed me in my eagerness for the church to join together and energize me to greater activism. And then Easter was on its way again. Easter is obviously a big cornerstone of the Christian church, and the pinnacle of the holy days, and here I was not yet on board with it. But on the laity side, in true Congregational, non-top-down style, a committee in some years creates a booklet for Lenten meditations, and I remember one they put together during that time. They collected from us favorite quotations, poems, and personal reflections for the booklet, one page for each day of the 40 days leading up to Easter. Those pages had glad revelations for me. There were some of my own stripe out there. One defined resurrection metaphorically as the reversal of what was thought to be final. The turning of midnight into dawn, hatred into love, dying into living anew. Abstract to be sure, but much more expansive than literalist thinking, and much easier for me to engage with, to chew on and live with compared with reciting a creed.

This was sweet, soft, river paddling. It prepared me to wait more patiently for a more head-on confrontation with the roiled waters of all that Easter stuff about Jesus dying for our sins. This was yet to come, at Easter 2016.

Early on, one of the kindred spirits I met at FCCB was Krista H. She'd led the Stewardship Board in 2010 and shared the story of her path to this place when she spoke about our August pledge drive. I want to tell a little of what she said because I appreciated her immensely, and because she'll reappear in these pages. In the 1970s she had a role in establishing a major wilderness set-aside here in Washington. Indeed, she radiates a heart that beats in time with forests and mountain snows. She called herself "in a way, an unlikely Christian. Not brought up in the church, I was not nurtured in its traditions, and the Bible did not give up its wisdom to me until later in life when literature opened me to the beauty of its language. In truth, my spiritual journey has been like that of a vagabond wandering through the faith traditions but never settling down. When God found me, it was often in solitary sojourns in the high desert where holiness took flight in sandhill cranes and glossy ibis. Then the sweet smell of sage after the rain seemed like heaven."

Continuing, Krista told us, "The world we live in is both beautiful and bewildering, simultaneously heart-breaking and life-affirming. We ask ourselves: How do we daily witness this brokenness and still walk with joy, adding our light and our love as all faith traditions teach us we must? This question has guided my life and helped me to see my need for a faith community, a spiritual home, a place where, together with others, I can do what in Hebrew is called '*tikkun olam*—the work of repairing the world.' For me, First Congregational Church of Bellingham is that place."

Under her leadership, the idea of stewardship expanded from taking care of the budget to taking better care of the Earth in our trust. Was this a signal that the church was ready to include Earth stewardship in all its stewardship? I hoped so.

8: Panama

Now that I had Christian credentials, I felt emboldened to follow my nostalgia for the youth group friends I knew as a ninth and tenth grader in the Panama Canal Zone. Across the years, I'd wished to renew these friendships, but felt the gulf between my fallen-away self and the Panama group was too big. At last I set out to find some of them and see where they were in life, and in religion. I had waited too long to do this, going on fifty years if that isn't just hilarious, but I was going to try. On the buffet next to the kitchen sits a black and white portrait of seven of us astride an ancient cannon on Taboga Island, just a short launch ride from the mainland. A lively composition of faces looks at Cito's camera: Tommy in a pair of wrap-around sunglasses that would still be cool today, paisley shorts on Lois, Miriam in a cotton print shirt I recognized as coming from the military Post Exchange because I had one like it, Tina in fitted white cut-off jeans, a straw hat tipped to reveal her big dark eyes and a small smile just tolerating this portrait sitting, and my secret crush Harry, impossibly Robert Redford handsome, sitting behind me (but going steady with Lois). Those seven and another dozen made up our high school youth group, a racial and ethnic mix, a four-year age range nobody minded, and I recall all of us tight as friends.

Aided by their unusual last name, I found the leaders of our old group—Jim and Hannah—I thought it likely they got married and went into the ministry. Sure enough, I found them at a church in the Midwest. I called the church. The secretary said, yes, they are still in the area, though retired from the ministry, and she was trusting enough to give me a phone number.

I spoke with Hannah. She seemed to remember me, and we delicately danced through some small talk, Hannah calling those years formative, and I could agree with that. I told her I was looking for my old best friend Becky, and Hannah tipped me off to a newsletter, "Panama Postscripts." The editor found Becky's sister in the Postscript's three-year-old directory, in Olympia, Washington—how close to me! Not locating a phone number, I wrote to her. The letter came back three weeks later, undeliverable. I subscribed to Postscripts, and looked for others in the group, and when the new directory came, with a new address for her, I re-sent my message and started to picture getting on Amtrak and going for a hearty reunion with Miriam and Becky. Though Miriam did call back, her news was that my friend Becky, who had been in Washington state for some years, now was moving to the Midwest with her family. I called right away, leaving a message for Becky—saying I still had her high school sophomore yearbook photo, and that on the back she'd written to not take too long to get in touch (the nature of a Canal Zone hitch was that we were most of us moving away). I spoke brightly of how it was a long time after all, but that I really would like to hear from her. She didn't call back. I was sad about that, but at least I'd tried.

A 2016 Panama Postscripts came, in which Hannah and Jim spoke of the blessing of knowing Reince Priebus, and what a deeply good Christian man he was, and how they were pinning their hopes on his ability to guide our new President. How anyone in high places in our nation's capital could have a reputation pure as snow with Hannah is a mystery to me. Certainly not any recent head of the Republican National Committee. Oh, well. If I thought, based on my current church experience, that much of the Christian world had moved quietly toward a more liberal theological stance, this reminded me, as the national news featured so relentlessly, that others had gone in the other direction.

This hope that one of their own evangelicals could have the ear of a leader, even, as some admitted, a very bad leader, turned out to be not unique to Hannah. Priebus, as we know, didn't last. But the hope didn't die.

In 2019, I would see an essay about Vice President Pence cast in the role, from the biblical book of Daniel, of counselor to a horrid king, going along with the bad administration while trying to steer it a bit. When a bit of nonsense crops up, a sociologist asks, how does it function? What does it do for the group? Presumably the example of Daniel served to remind folks of their group identity, for starters. Moreover, while nonsensical to those outside the group, this framing must have functioned to tamp down criticism of their baffling stance from inside their ranks. All so that their long-range purpose could inch forward in the obscuring foam.

That aside, my attempts to contact Panama Canal Zone friends got me thinking how right Hannah was in calling our Panama time formative. I was fifteen and growing up, and Panama was more than an exotic backdrop to my life then. Dad had gone ahead of us. Mom had the tasks of storing furniture and arranging with a property management firm for care of our house, and shepherding us all through passports and tropical shots—yellow fever and so on. She had bought a used little bug of a car, a mid-1950s Nash, for her own little Tacoma run-around car, and it gave signs of a cracked block. Rather than chuck the car, she replaced the engine, deciding to keep it for use in Panama. Mom, her three girls, and Grandma Winnie squeezed into this little car for the January cross-country trip to Charleston, SC. Since I was too young to drive, Grandma's job was to help Mom drive the long trek. My job was to re-load the luggage every morning from whatever motel, re-fitting it like an interlocking puzzle into the small trunk. Mom planned a longer southerly route aimed at avoiding snow and ice. Even so, January asserted itself and we had a forced layover in the Texas panhandle until a blizzard passed. At Charleston, we took Grandma to the airport to jet home, turned the car over to the shippers, and boarded our own flight on an old military prop plane.

The four of us emerged squinting against the Panamanian sun, and immediately felt the assault of the heavy, soggy air. Welcome to Panama, where we slowed to a languid shuffle across the tarmac to the waiting intake office.

Dad's position as a civilian auditor working for the U.S. Army placed us in a curious status between officers and enlisteds. We would be welcomed into the privilege of Monday night supper at the Officers Club, spiffing up each week for the stately drive down a palm-lined causeway to the club, but we were housed with a more humble underclass.

From the airfield, Dad drove us along a spacious main avenue through Balboa, where we passed one-story concrete houses, painted white and dressed with native palms in neat front garden strips. The window glass was curiously sectioned, and Dad explained those were louvers. I saw that the glass louvers were in closed position—air conditioning was on. These houses looked comfortable.

"Is our house like these?" I asked.

"Those are officers' quarters," Dad said, "We're almost to our place."

Soon we came to Curundu, and Dad pulled the car beneath a thin wooden building raised as if on stilts, the carport sharing shade with clothes lines and what-not. We tramped up the staircase to investigate our new digs.

"Dad, I'm hot. Turn on the air conditioning."

"Dad, the windows have no glass."

"We'll have breezes instead of air conditioning. See, the louvers open to screens." Dad liked the tropics.

Mom had worked in Florida during WWII and was more or less prepared to make an adventure out of Panama. And she did. Schooldays, she tapped into the waning indigenous culture, making tracings at the library from which she painted formalized designs on mahogany plates that hung on her walls the rest of her life. She also never forgot her trip to the the San Blas Islands, world-famous for their inverse appliqué work. In the tiny green Nash, which arrived after long weeks of waiting, she took us kids on weekend trips, checking out highway markers, gawking at the jungle where we could spot a sloth that moved even more slowly than its reputation, and stopping at roadside fruit stands where we bought mango and papaya.

In many outward ways, Panama Canal Zone life was simple for me. When the trucks spraying DDT rumbled down our street, never with any warning, we leapt to close our wooden louvers to keep out as much of the stinky cloud as we could. The international high school was air conditioned, except for outdoor physical education (I remember field hockey) that left me dripping with sweat even after showering, only to shiver in my especially cold Biology class. I think they were trying to keep dissection specimens cool.

We shopped in the sparsely stocked Post Exchange for consumer goods—I remember the first time through I couldn't find a swimming suit to fit. My high school Spanish wasn't good enough to lead Mom and my sisters into Panama City on our own, but we drove to what was called the interior and negotiated in Spanish with a nearly toothless man for a barrel-sized rough-woven basket. I still have it and use it, though the lid has long since had it.

The Canal Zone lacked department stores, or big stores of any kind. We had a good sewing machine and sewed our own clothes when we couldn't find something to suit. We started with simple cotton caftans and muumuus. Then I sewed church outfits. Although no one makes her own clothes anymore, sewing had its satisfactions. You work with whole cloth to produce exactly what you envision. Or something reasonably close to your vision. In so many areas of our lives we don't have that—we work in existing businesses, we raise kids with the help of existing quirky adults, we get dental work that accommodates what's already there, we vote on policies that seek to rebalance previous policies. But sewing provides step-by-step satisfaction, from fabric on the bolt to end result. Maybe it's no coincidence that when home sewing fell away, knitting and crafting jumped. We need to create. All of us. I love that men have their basement and garage shops, even "man sheds" for building and socializing. Creative time has often been termed an escape, but it's much more than that. It puts us in touch with what is elemental in being human. It's an experience that can be touched by grace. Or Grace.

We could walk to the little church in Curundu. Many in the youth group were bilingual and I got to Panama City occasionally with church friends. I even got into a casino when still fifteen, and was allowed to play the slots. A nod and a wink instead of an ID check.

Despite the church's modest Quonset hut structure—a military-surplus corrugated steel half-cylinder served by a small air conditioning unit that couldn't keep up—the entire congregation of the Curundu Community Church dressed up for Sunday. I was especially proud of a two-piece dress in a shell-pink polyester crepe de chine—a lined slim skirt, the top a blouson style lightly gathered into a stiffened bottom collar fitted to the top of the hip. I hoped to emulate Audrey Hepburn's elegance—"Charade" had come out in 1963. I think of how we sang "Onward Christian Soldiers" while we looked like we were going to a garden party and certainly had nothing to fight about, let alone "marching as to war." I got mildly nauseous and didn't know why this hymn affected me that way. But it had something to do with the severely drawn fence from other groups, the looking for enemies, the militarism.

53

A family dynamic plays in here. My trip down memory lane veers into the weeds, and I sit at my keyboard and find I am peeling back another layer of the onion of my formation. It was in Panama that a fault line of my upbringing brought a quake. It came at the beginning, when Mom and my sisters and I arrived in the Panama Canal Zone, six months after Dad had gone to start his elective two-year tour of duty. Just as quickly as the heavy Panamanian air hit us, Mom found that Dad had consorted with a local woman those entire six months. Not only that, but this fact was known by his boss and throughout the social circle Mom was stepping into. I was fifteen, in the second half of ninth grade. Mom had no friends there yet. She knew eighteen long months stretched ahead of us. Mom made me her confidante. She was upset, but oddly less shocked than I expected, and seemed to fairly quickly feel better after having laid this on me. I mostly kept intact my relationship with my father, in a pretense that I didn't know what I knew. Things settled, Mom found some bosom buddies to spend days with, Mom and Dad gradually mended their rift. But my world was badly torn, and I bottled up my hurt.

And before Panama? My mother, of course, raised me to be a good woman and daughter. She taught me to put family first: make a loving home, make nutritious meals (soda pop and white bread were rare). Endure, find friends, and control what you can control. Follow the rules, be prepared, vigilant, practical. Let God guide conscience. On the other hand, my father wasn't content that I be a good daughter. He wanted a surrogate son as well. He groomed me to be in some ways like a good man of the times, able to stand alone and apart. Like him, I tucked my feelings away, made reasoning my method, and avoided embarrassments like the plague. By fifth grade my father and I were regularly discussing the latest issue of *Scientific American*, and when he got home from the office I eagerly jabbered to him about my day at school, sometimes even before he had a chance to hang up his suit and get into his fatigues. By sixth grade, we were plotting what courses I'd take, what foreign language to study to get ready for college. He admired the pith of ancient Greek philosophy: Moderation in all things. Structure, Harmony, and Proportion. Let the mind govern. It was much later, after I was an adult, that he spilled the pap that he had absorbed somewhere and still believed: The intellect is superior to emotions, emotions are a vestige of the "mammalian brain." Females are stuck in that earlier mammalian brain (!), ergo, they are not to be heeded. The exception he allowed for his daughters' intelligence did not disturb this rule.

That's the humorous part of this rumination, although it was more humorous before certain factions in our society started making headway in their aims to drag women back to 1910. The flip side of Dad's mental universe—that emotions in men are to be suppressed as unworthy of their superior status—surely harmed all of us in our little five-member family.

In our childhood, Dad's emotions came out in spite of his philosophy. No surprise there. From time to time, Dad erupted in anger. And Julie was the lightning rod who received Dad's anger. So much for moderation in all things. Mom didn't usually stand up to him. Julie's response was to harden up about it, not yielding her integrity, bless her. I turned my confused feelings against myself.

Many decades after Panama, my new wider family in my Congregational church had helped nurture me, sort of like re-parenting me. One day Julie and I found the table was set for the two of us to pour out experiences that we'd separately kept bottled up. If we thought we were pretty close before, simply with different personalities, now we have a closeness that is too precious to describe.

The writer of "Onward Christian Soldiers," Sabine Baring-Gould, may have believed he was just writing an innocent children's march to join with the children of another village, as he said in a statement. He said he wrote it quickly, overnight while hardly thinking about it. He couldn't even see the militarism in it—"mighty army," "into battle," "against the foe." Who is the foe here? Other religions? Perhaps anyone who might speak out against colonialism? Written at a time, 1864, when the British were flush with colonial triumph, he and his apologists tried to explain away the apparent militarism. But children would be absorbing the message into their own forming minds. How could they not?

However, if this old march was useful in the 1960s Civil Rights movement, as I'm told, then it did have value. Sometimes you do have to focus on the dangers of enemies, and sometimes you do have to warrior up. But I'm glad "We Shall Overcome" became more iconic to the movement. I won't ever *like* "Onward"—it asks those who sing it to consider themselves to be in a permanent army, and to me that is a difference in attitude, like between learning how to shoot a rifle, as Dad taught Julie and me at the Curundu Gun Club, versus carrying one around all the time.

9: A Matinee Idol Arrives

Kent French came from the East Coast to become FCCB's permanent lead pastor in 2012. A dynamo. A beautiful singing voice. A matinee idol's dark, wavy hair. A storyteller to rival Broadway, and no notes, all from memory. Things began to change.

New young families began trickling in to Sunday service. Where once babies had been so few they were swarmed on Sundays, their parents effusively congratulated, now children became a welcome commonplace. The smallest children provided a chorus during the service. We might be in a brief lull between a hymn and the next speaker mounting the steps to the pulpit, and an "Arr-oww!" would ring out, a baby testing his lungs, sounding like a crow. Or in the midst of the sermon might come an owlet's "Wooo" or a high small shriek, hawk-like. In the speaker-equipped Narthex, rocking chairs grew in number, occupied more often than not by parents able to watch through the Sanctuary's windows if their progeny was too vocal. Inside the Sanctuary, a stack of floor cushions and bags of small amusements took over a corner among yet more rocking chairs.

For me, Kent brought the promise of new projects in addition to membership growth. He told us one Sunday, "Our faith is 2,000 years old, but our thinking is not." And he asked, only partly rhetorically, "What is our unique calling?" He wanted us to think about that seriously. I rubbed my hands together, hungry for going deeper into change, together.

One Sunday in the late fall, I crossed Cornwall at a trot to arrive at the top of the stairs at 9:55. Opening the door, for at this time of year, Advent, the doors were no longer propped wide open as in summer, I nodded at the greeters whom I'd soon get to. I hung up my parka in the coat alcove, unclipped my name badge from one of the wide red ribbons anchored on the wall for this purpose. Felt for a collar edge to clasp it to and shook hands with the greeters, now with the easy confidence of being a member and knowing them. Moving through the Narthex, for that was what the "courtyard" was called, I noticed that the air was free of strong perfumes, and wondered why I hadn't noticed this absence before. How nice, and was it happenstance or on purpose? I exchanged greetings with people whose faces had become familiar, and as usual, entered the Sanctuary at the third door, where I accepted the day's bulletin from an usher.

I sat down beside an acquaintance, Lynn D., a widow a little older than I, with merry eyes. We enjoyed the syncopation in the opening hymn, turning to each other once to smile at it. The opening was led by a teenager at the pulpit: "A poet once said, 'Live the questions now.'" Following along, the congregation read aloud, "And so we have come with our questions."

The teen continued the familiar call and response pattern—in the bulletin, regular typeface for the liturgist, boldface for the congregation's response. I liked the part where we said "A constant presence." God doesn't have to be human-like, with eyeballs looking over your shoulder—there are other types of presences, and I wondered how others in the pews conceived of God. I could *enjoy* this approach to belief. Imagine, actually enjoying religion!

Then Kent said, "In place of a sermon this Sunday, Tara and I will answer any and all questions." Tara was Tara Olsen, the second pastor, also from the East Coast, who'd joined us about the same time as Kent. I glanced at Lynn, my mouth in O form, and her face echoed the same surprise at this without-a-net bravery.

I had missed the previous Sunday, as had Lynn, when they collected questions, which had gone under lock and key out of reach of the pastors. Now a slip was drawn from a basket. The first question was tame. The second question, however, was a bit of a jolt.

"Does it matter whether what is written in the Bible is true or not?"

Can you *do* that? Can you ask that, out loud? Lynn and I looked at one another. I saw her eyebrows were raised—she was thinking the same thing I was.

Tara and Kent chuckled in good humor, and Kent took this one. "The Bible is true. And some of it actually happened." A strong ripple of laughter burbled from the congregation. "Over time, unlike during the time of oral traditions, we have come to equate truth with fact," Kent said easily, without needing to blot his brow with his folded white handkerchief the way he did during a typical sermon. "But to hold the Bible to factualness is to do it injustice. *The Grapes of Wrath* is true. George Washington chopping down the cherry tree is true, whether it is factual or not."

My, this isn't my mother's Christianity. Not my childhood Christianity at all.

And on it went, with some softball questions and some zingers. I listened while the second pastor, Tara, added, "What *you* bring to your reading also matters. Adopt the belief that helps you love God. The virgin birth? If it troubles you, why not focus on the question of whether there's a virgin spot in you where God wants to be born."

Lynn and I smiled broadly at each other. We would each start our week relaxed and spiritually fed. And I began to see how this church's welcome extends to those who are presently staying out of church, going it alone with their spiritualality. They, too, could comfortably come to a church that gives them spiritual prompts, homework aimed at deepening and sweetening their journey.

10: Wherein I Visit a Fox News Church

E ven evangelicals have no monolithic unity. I thought they did, wielding militaristic discipline to keep their ranks stiffly strong and apparently inured to what secular humanists see as social justice. So I was surprised when I heard of evangelical churches demonstrating against mountaintop-removal mining in the eastern U.S. Could there be a crossing of the divide of conservative and progressive churches via a joint action on the climate?

I visited a Baptist church in town one year during Advent, foregoing FCCB's service that Sunday to learn what a local Baptist church might be doing about Earth stewardship. If an evangelical church in the eastern U.S. had protested mountaintop removal by a mining company, even going on site to link hands in witness, I wondered what a possibly similar church here might be doing, and whether our churches could do something together. Watched from the lot all the way in to the foyer, I saw my answer. Their bulletin board covered a wall, all about their foreign missions to spread The Word, nothing about any other concern. I guess we won't be doing anything jointly on the environment. I suppose it was a naive hope.

From a tight doorway to one side a man in a suit sailed toward me and showed me into the social room he'd come from. Several others sought to welcome me and offer coffee. The suited man even glad-handed me like the old stereotype of a life insurance agent. Welcoming, but with an agenda. You know how in your body you feel the difference between a genuine welcome and a lure? Call me suspicious, but that's what I felt: a lure. I was stuck now to stay for the service.

In the service, I was surprised there was no mention of the season anywhere—not a Christmas carol among the hymns, nor a mention of seasonal activities, nor any nod to Advent in the sermon. Just repeated exhortations to be sure you and those you meet are saved, and stay saved. Warnings against backsliding. And lots of references to blood. I hasten to add that this isn't a portrait of all Baptist churches, and much later I sat in Hovander Park north of Bellingham with a woman who is a member of another Baptist church. She said her church does indeed mark the Advent season. She seemed familiar with the reputation of the one I had visited. I saw her draw her mouth in slightly. She said hers was different. I was glad to hear that.

The neglect of Christmas I'd found at the one church provoked me in light of what national evangelical political leadership was trumpeting. I wonder if the members of the Baptist church I sat with, while neglecting the advent of Christmas themselves, were among those riled up by Fox News and by certain evangelical flame-throwers to believe that the mainstream culture had mounted a "war on Christmas." If they were truly upset, then where was their support for and reverence for Christmas?

The "war" brouhaha was, of course, not really about whether it was better to use the greeting "Happy Holidays" over "Merry Christmas." As an issue, that was actually pretty easy to resolve. In inventing a nonexistent war and accusing others of waging it against them, these firebrands knew it would serve their purposes to make use of the awful connotations of real warfare. How better to stir their followers than a call to arms, translated into votes they could direct and mainstream media they could villainize. A couple of years later, I saw that this same local church's website had given prominent space to a vitriolic—and incoherent—anti-Muslim campaign by one of their members. I hope readers will forgive me for suspecting what goes with what.

But conservative and anti-Muslim do not necessarily go together. Conservative churches are, at least in some places, welcoming the stranger. I was surprised by an example here in Washington State in January of 2016, when the new administration first declared a travel ban on Islamic immigrants, a decision supposedly catering to conservative Christians as well as other anti-immigrant factions. Seattle-area evangelicals were among the most shocked and appalled. The *Seattle Times* columnist Danny Westneat interviewed distraught workers at Washington's largest refugee resettlement program, a charity run by a coalition of mostly evangelical churches that self-identify as conservative. They told Westneat they took large exception to the new Administration's assertion that immigrants had been coming in unvetted. Moreover, they loved the immigrants they'd been able to help, most definitely including the Muslims.

11: A Raucous Christmas Pageant

Our 2012 children's Christmas pageant was one for the ages. It tickles me still in light of a later Advent with our subsequent pastor, Sharon Benton. Sharon is a mix of matronly strength and almost teen-like vulnerability, a mixture of great charm when the shorter layers of her long haircut fall into her eyes,. She did the Time with Children segment on a Sunday in December, 2016. Sharon gathered the children down front and unpacked a nativity scene on the Communion table, with stuffed figures that didn't really want to stand up. She fussed over placing each piece, and said it had to be perfect. Once placed, the figures couldn't be touched, none allowed to fall over. Then she dropped the pretense and made her point: Keeping faith with the Christmas story didn't actually mean keeping it perfect and apart from us. Rather, all children are loved by God and can touch and help in church. YOU are part of the story, she told the rapt children.

What Sharon didn't know was that we adults had already lived and laughed the truth of her words in the pageant of 2012. Since Sharon had not been part of FCCB then, I should tell her about it.

The pageant director was Sharry Nyberg, our long-time children's minister, who couldn't be more loved by the children (or us adults), now or in any year. She had worked for weeks with the kids and coordinated with the choir director and home seamsters. The children were costumed as shepherds, wise men, angels, sheep, and of course, a star. A little face peered out from a center hole in the five-point gold star that otherwise encased her down to her knees. Sewn from stiff foam-backed fabric, the shiny star provided our first chuckle as the points bent with each jerk of a restless elbow inside. The shape sprang back, and then distorted again with the child's next fidget. Twinkle, twinkle, little star?

Church secretary Kathryn T. and her husband sat at center, done up as Mary and Joseph, their nine-month-old baby standing in for baby Jesus. Rising behind them was the familiar brown plinth with its slim glass cross lit by the 10:00 a.m. daylight from the hidden window. Now, however, it looked not like a cross on a backdrop but like a sueded gift box snugged with a silvery ribbon. Soloists including Kent placed themselves around the crèche scene, and sang the story. Sharry directed and encouraged from the first pew, front right, a two-year-old boy sitting on her knee.

I sat three pews back from Sharry and noticed the two-year-old hop down from her lap and take a couple of steps toward the center scene. She quietly motioned him back. He returned to her side, hovering. But as the songs moved the story along, Sharry could no longer keep the boy with her. Soon I saw why. Having his parents in a clear line of sight wasn't sufficient for the little guy. He broke, trotting to the front . . . and climbed up onto Joseph's lap.

Laughter erupted from the pews, but the holy family didn't break form. So, *ahem*, Jesus seems to have an older brother. A bit inconvenient for the story but awfully cute.

Next a small "sheep" bolted away. Halfway down the center aisle he reconsidered, tuned to some unseen cue. He stood and picked his nose. Then when it dawned on him that he was immune to capture, the adults remaining glued in place, he turned and ran to his grandmother standing at the back, to a second wave of chuckles all around.

Now the small wise ones proceeded down the aisle, made up with greasepaint facial hair drawn fancifully, a curled mustache on one, mutton chops on another, a beard on the third. One little boy, whom I knew to have been adopted from Ethiopia, played his part solemnly. Small with gorgeous fine features, he was no more than four years old. Dangling from his little hand was a brass pot, obviously heavy for him, but he held his grip. His perfect maroon velveteen robe was tied with a gilt rope. Silvery beads cascaded to his waist. He approached, then slowed, suddenly uncertain, for baby Jesus had gone wiggly.

Mary lifted little Jesus from her lap and settled him onto the floor on his belly. Our Ethiopian wise man, mollified, delivered his gift to Mary. Hardly a beat later, a roar of laughter erupted in the first rows. I leaned to peer around those in front of me, and followed the gaze of the laughers all the way to the floor. And then I was laughing, too.

Behold a Christmas miracle! Jesus, the newborn, rolled himself to his feet. And walked!

12: Head Trips

After finding that progressive churches have a lot to offer, I nevertheless completely respect the choice of an increasing number of Americans who are content living without religion in their lives. Still, I think some well-rounded familiarity with Christianity can be liberating, and can offer a window into aspects of our secular culture.

Christianity simply has ongoing strong effects that refuse to stay on the page, and refuse to stay inside the church. Effects that slide into or reinforce our secular culture. For one, when we are sure we have found an enemy, a group we think we need to fight against, we demonize them. If scholar Elaine Pagels is right, demonization came in with Christianity and wasn't really present before. The leap is from the simpler concept of the enemy, the Other, to the enemy as demon. I didn't have to be curious about religion scholars to find this. Simply as a reader of *The New Yorker* I was familiar with essayist David Remnick, so when he wrote about Dr. Pagels' life and work, I took a look. He writes, "For Pagels, demonization is a crucial and terrifying component of Christianity. What began as a minority sect's rhetorical strategy, a way of defining and asserting itself, became a majority religion's moral, and even psychological, justification for persecution: first of Jews, then of

Romans and of heretics—of all opponents, real or imagined."[1] You know this habit of mind has gone broadly cultural when you see that atheists have absorbed it, too. Sure, cultural influences go both ways between religion and the secular, but it's good to know how far back some things go. And now we have, maybe globally, vicious Twitter swarms, and cancel culture. I hope I never get in the crosshairs of such a swarm.

To try to ignore titanic religious influences just drives them below the conscious level, where it is surely more difficult to deal with them. For me personally, trying to dismiss the Christian religion, as I used to, had the effect of weakening my sense of ancestry and my understanding of my own formation. Not to mention tripping over the lumps in my carpet from many sweepings-under of religious ideas I didn't want to think about. So like many other Americans, I haven't always known what I didn't know, or even have well-formed questions. I "knew" that Christianity was a sour mix of contradictions: inspirational comforts on the one hand, and hurtfulness on the other—toward women, toward care of our Earth, and toward other religions. So, all those years ago, I moved on. Yet, as I saw how we as a modern culture did likewise about many things—moving on—I was frustrated at how we fall into the trap of ignoring our common herd frailties in favor of a pop psychology that implies that all failure is the individual's personal failure. So, then we chase the next bright star and self-help guru that offers individual solutions.

Unaware at the outset of my quest of the recent decades of scholarly theological, historical and textual research, I didn't know what thrills were in store for me. Not nerdy detail, but shattering findings from such prominent scholars as Elaine Pagels. As another example, at one time, she says, the Adam and Eve story was a parable of human freedom.[2] Stunning! That changed in the fourth century to the now familiar story of inherent sinfulness. What else might be lying in plain sight, or maybe only obscured beneath the frothy surface until the paddle catches hold of the firm water beneath?

---

1. Remnick, *Devil Problem*, 204.

2. Pagels, *Adam, Eve, and the Serpent.*

13: Beach Spirit

U p to this point, I was soaking up this new version of Christianity with
my head. And gradually, with my emotions, too, and I was enjoying
moments of peace and comfort. It was okay with me that, likely, I wouldn't
also find a mountaintop religious experience. I was content just to reduce
anxious thoughts, reduce my irritable charging about. I had for quite some
time used a thought for the day to reset myself as needed, an orientation
to return to when I got off in the blackberry brambles of my mental path.
Because, like a dog, I seem to need something to chew on. Giving my mind
a key thought is a way of saying "Here, girl, chew on this instead." I gleaned
a number of orienting thoughts from Hugh Prather's 1986 workbook on
happiness, such as, "Today I will judge nothing that occurs,"[1] and had begun to use a book of koans, John Tarrant's *Bring Me the Rhinoceros*, riddles
to mull with his guidance. Koans provide prompts into poet Rainer Maria
Rilke's famous and wonderful phrase, "live the question."

I forget what question, affirmation, or riddle I was pondering when,
in a cold March week, Bill and I went on a short getaway to the Olympic
Peninsula and the ocean. We stayed in a cabin that delighted us with honey-
colored log walls and wood stove warmth. The beaches just north of Kalaloch

1. Prather, *How to Live*, 68.

were sparsely visited, no doubt due to the cold and wind—I needed two coats and two hats. However, the solitude did invite lengthy strolls, and over about three days we explored four nearby beaches, separated from each other by headlands. Each one different from the last, and each with its own charms. Sometimes we found ourselves completely alone—we could have owned the beach, and Bill and I remarked to each other on this.

Perhaps it was in this spirit of ownership that I had the impulse to pick up a little around the place. Bits of colored plastic scalloped the surf line on the grayish, cloud-shadowed beach. Larger bits farther up the beach came into view when you got close enough. On that cloudy, breezy day with fresh ocean scents in our noses, it seemed a fine thing to do to pick up some of the larger pieces, and soon my hands were full.

For our second walk, after a lunch and a warming by a crackling fire, we chose a beach a bit further north, called Beach 4. We wondered how they could have run out of names, tagging a nice beach with just a number. This time I came equipped with a bag that came to hand from our food stores in the kitchenette. Just a flimsy one like you bring home a vegetable in. At first glance I didn't think there would be a need for my bag. This beach looked pristine and intriguing. Up close, however, I saw lengths of rope, the inexpensive yellow polypro you can get anywhere. Some was half buried, and too much for my little bag. But Bill joined in, and soon I saw I enjoyed this as much as I'd ever enjoyed agate-hunting on Oregon's beaches.

I had long known of the harm of plastics loose in the ocean, how they not only kill when they fill the stomachs of marine life, but are toxic even when degraded to the molecular level. But there seemed no need to think deeply about this. We simply gathered our catch in the contentment of being there.

Nearby Ruby Beach was next. Gorgeous rock towers off shore, remnants of ancient headlands. This time with a little larger receptacle, a sturdy bread bag. We collected a diabolical wad of filament and hooks, as well as yet more plastic fragments in crayon colors red, white, and blue. This was plentifully absorbing, the spotting, the picking up. A man took notice of our haul and chatted with us about it. The long bread bag filled up to bursting.

That our accomplishment was gratifying was no surprise. But then I noticed what was sneaking up on me. It was more than satisfaction.

Imperceptibly, I began to feel like I wasn't really *on* the beach like an owner; now I felt invited to be *of* the beach. Or *in* the beach—in some way part of the beach itself. There really aren't words for this. Without conscious intent, I slipped into my place within this place. Inanimate stones had a sheen of ocean water, of course, but also a sheen of . . . I hesitate to say, *friendliness,* as though what I saw bypassed my mind and went straight to my spirit. And when my back started to ache, the beach seemed to cluck in sympathy, and the ache felt better, like a mother's kiss on a scraped knee. These were moments that seemed out of time. Eternal in a way. In these moments—did it last an hour?—as the boundaries of my self expanded and became permeable, I was deeply, quietly happy. A presence, as I call it, does not require personification. The afterglow of happiness lasted the rest of the trip and beyond. The memory remains like a song to me. A mountaintop in a beach pebble.

I continue to wonder about this experience. On my walks now, I listen for this sense of happy belonging, whether on rare trips to the beach, or more commonly in the forest, or on my street. If this is what's in store when I live with a question, any work that results won't feel dutiful. It will be happy work.

Happy work—that in itself is some sort of breakthrough from how oxymoronic those two words are to me when put together. Too often work has been something to bear down on, more or less tensely, and get done in order to earn relaxation time, so the prospect of happy work sparks a new and free attitude.

Could it be that when anything is looked at from the mind of I-Thou rather than I-It, that God is there, too? We whites tend to find indigenous religious thought alien, animist. But I think I just stepped closer to them. And closer to Judaism as well, in its refusal to name God and thereby to avoid slipping, however slightly, into making an object of God. Ironically, I was finding more insight and happiness by burrowing deeper into one faith, even as it led me to find kinship with other faiths. I can see why the Dalai Lama had this answer for a seeker: the woman asked if she should leave Christianity for Buddhism, and he told her she should stay and become the best Christian she could. Not because it was better, but because going further on a good path is what it's all about. I thank him for that.

Feeling actively part of a place, as I did on that beach, was an experience that gave me a better base for my religious practice—it is one thing to have a conception of something, and that often comes first, but having an experience like this helped me find a core place in myself, a welcoming home base. Though of course I am a citizen of the U.S., day to day I've habitually been more a citizen of the country of the mind, accustomed to ranging far and wide. Not a bad thing, except that I treated actual places like scaffolding for what I thought of as larger purposes. The actual place of my house was like a support pod that fed and sheltered me in a way that I could take for granted, so that I—that is, my mind—could go roaming, either solo, or share my roamings with friends, who shared theirs with me. Now I'm more place-based. At least, more place-aware and appreciative. I like what the late Sam Shepard, playwright and actor, told an interviewer about the commonplace notions of individual identity. He said that having a strong sense of self isn't believing in a lot. To me, this is not saying anything against protecting the individual in our society, her creativity, his self-expression, her independent thought, their self-reliance. Rather, it illuminates a prime cause of the loneliness we feel when our selfhood borders are so crisp and well-defended we are unable to feel belonging. Real places now seem crucial to my happiness. Is that important? Is happiness frivolous? I find that nurturing my happiness is the only way I can be reliably kind. Thank you, Hugh Prather, who found this to be true for himself and centered it in his workbook, guiding me to experience it for myself.

14: Birthday Eco-Present

A rriving back at home from the coast that March, we saw that the Indian Plum, or Osoberry as we know it, had been busy leafing out. No longer the lichen-festooned, brushy, dead-looking branches we'd left behind but the first harbinger of spring. My birthday was coming. I flirted with the idea of getting myself an electric tricycle like my friend Joyce Jimerson used for local trips instead of a car. She offered hers for a try-out, so Bill and I drove the two miles over to Joyce's. We drove up the steep slope of their gravel driveway and parked to the side of the garage. Her garage door was already open and she greeted us with her trademark infectious cheer, her long, light-brown hair always in the same loose twist pinned at the back of her head Earth-mother style, a few frizzles floating free.

"Good morning! I was just feeding the ducks," she said.

"Can we see?"

She walked us through the breezeway between garage and house, a shady spot infused with a relaxed green coziness. Very near the house was the vegetable garden, inexpensively fenced off from the ducks (and deer). The ducks, which produce eggs of prodigious size and flavor, had their own wander-way among shrubs and crabapple trees on a slope. A compact yard, full of interesting things, it included a pair of cisterns, painted a light rusty brown to match the house. In the dry summer months, the over 600 gallons of reserve rainwater make the vegetables grow.

But I was there to ride her tricycle, a grown-up tricycle, heavy, sturdy, with the front stretched out to make long legs comfortable, but the design had you upright, not recumbent. The wheel pattern was reversed from the child's version—the two wheels were in front, and the rider sat just forward of the single wheel in back. When I remarked on this, she said this configuration had been found to be more stable. I already knew the first "why" of the tricycle. A vehicle with four wheels and power makes it a motor vehicle subject to licensing and all that.

Joyce wheeled the bright yellow contraption out of the garage and showed me the hand controls for power and brakes. I could pedal it with leg power, and add a power boost at will. I was excited, already picturing myself on my own tricycle zipping forward from a stop sign to the surprise of drivers behind me expecting me to be slow. I sat at the ready and surveyed the terrain in front of me with a moment's trepidation; I saw slope, gravel, and turns no matter which way I might choose. But with two sets of eyes on me, and Joyce and Bill falling silent, waiting, I chose not to face the main drive right off, whose long slope down to the road seemed daunting before I'd even had a chance to test the brakes on gravel, so instead I picked a little path that swung around the far side of the garage. But it meant turning across the up-slope.

"Here goes nothing!" I said.

And promptly ten feet later, braking and trying to lean upslope, I slowly tipped over down-slope. I lay there, sharp gravel grinding into a knee, the weight of the thing trapping me, and my first thought was, have I chipped the paint on Joyce's $5,000 tricycle? Or worse?

My second thought was the one I spoke aloud, "Well? Help me up! What are you waiting for? Bill?"

"Are you all right?" said Joyce.

"Oh, yeah, I'm coming," Bill said. "I just couldn't believe my eyes." And he let out a rueful and slightly suppressed chuckle.

Of course I said I was all right, even though I wasn't sure. I was bumped, scraped, and bruised, and I'd made a mess of this tryout. A tricycle was not for me. At least I hadn't damaged it, or not so we noticed.

The cisterns now looked darned attractive. Bill bought me a 305-gallon, food-grade black plastic above-ground cistern like Joyce's, which we installed nestled on a tiny terrace a few steps down from our back patio.

We could stand below and turn on the spigot, which was of course near the bottom of the broad barrel. No crouching down. I thought that was pretty clever. A cute little set-up that harvests water from the back side of the roof. It makes our home, our little spot, seem more complete unto itself. Integrated with the gifts of nature, instead of shunting away water as soon as it falls, then buying it back after chlorine and other treatment just in order to water the nearby fern bed and ornamentals in summer.

Joyce and I remain friends, of course, despite my endangering her expensive tricycle. She even joined our church choir. Not due to any fine Christian light shining from me, nor to being asked, but simply out of her desire to do more singing, and my telling her you don't have to be a church member to sing in our choir.

15: Earth Day: My Turn in the Pulpit

We had been doing small things toward environmental problems for some time. In 2010 an active, soft-spoken member, Rob O., initiated a Green Team, with me as his shadow co-chair, to promote environmental awareness and action. The first meetings garnered a lot of attendance, maybe eighteen of us. There was Neal N., who was interested in the scriptural underpinnings of Earth stewardship. And Tony, whose passion was healing war veterans through organic farming. Sherry, who wanted to get carpooling to church started. Helen M., who had gleaned for years for the food bank, and would soon be sewing cloth grocery bags for the local push to ban the plastic ones.

Then the next autumn, 2011, I undertook Carbon Master volunteer training through the Washington State University Extension office. Carbon Masters was a pilot program modeled on Master Gardeners, to prepare volunteers for public education roles about climate change. In classroom lectures by experts from universities in Washington and British Columbia, we learned we were moving headlong toward some horrific disaster scenarios, with the oceans already having absorbed from the atmosphere pretty much all they *can* absorb from decades of fossil fuel burning, and the hurts were showing now, not in the distant future.

We also learned how paradoxically difficult it was going to be to galvanize action, even though there was quiet work underway, such as by the Washington State University agriculture researchers. Our leader for the ten weeks was my friend Joyce Jimerson, the ebullient and very funny Master Composter and keeper of ducks, yet even her natural high spirits did not protect her from a bout of despair and depression over the enormity of the coming problems. It was good to have company in my personal reactions, and low spirits didn't stop us from pushing forward. What projects would the ten of us like to devise? Joyce suggested we start where we were already affiliated. Well, for me that was church. And so, with Rob prepared to lead, I proposed projects to our Green Team, while the church maintenance committee retrofitted our building for energy conservation.

The Green Team opted to plan a boffo Earth Day service for April 2012, and we were given almost the entire hour-long Sunday service to design to this theme—music to sermon to benediction.

Mark Schofield and I volunteered to take the sermon time. We met for coffee, finding quiet in the skinny ell of the Village Books coffee shop on the third floor, where west-facing windows gave us a view of the March chop on Bellingham Bay. We needed to hammer out a plan for tandem sermonettes, reflections, as they are called in this church when laity take the pulpit. We were working well ahead, more than a month out. That is, well ahead for Mark, barely ahead for my comfort. The theme the planning group chose was "gratitude for the Earth," so as to gently pull listeners in to our message and not preach at them. I suspected that this congregation largely left to others any focused action on the climate crisis in their admittedly admirable concentration on human services and social justice. But Mark and I could model some of what we'd like to see the church do. Somehow we would cover energy and paper usage using the gratitude idea.

We sidled into our task and learned we each had memorable times at Lutheran summer camps. He'd been to a camp in Colorado while in high school. I had been to Holden Village on Lake Chelan in Washington, just for an inexpensive vacation with my husband and niece.

"Mark, you know how when we have reflections, they are each on the theme, but they are separate. Could we instead set this up as a conversation?" I noticed I was leaning forward and sweeping the tabletop, my ambitions getting me excited. I broke off a piece of my scone, trying to quiet myself so Mark could react to the idea rather than my intensity.

"If we can pull it off," Mark said, his deep, sandy voice calm and steady. "But I may not be able to get to writing my part for a while, with work the way it is. Maybe we can use those Lutheran camp remembrances to link our parts together. If I take paper usage and you take the Community Energy Challenge, we'll have two scripts that we should be able to turn into a back-and-forth later." We agreed to work separately and then meet again.

All of the other parts of the service were likewise coming together. Several of us from Green Team met with Tara. We chose hymns, Tara would write a prayer to suit, Wendy would take the Time with Children and get Western Red Cedar seedlings to give out. Mark gathered facts on our church paper-usage from Kathryn in the office, and, with Emily's artistry for the cover, I designed a honed-down bulletin for the service, using just one sheet of paper instead of three. We hoped it could be a model, or at least a demo of what is possible without destroying the breathing room for the eye, the "white space" that readers need.

Then it was time to run our plan by Kent. I met with him for permission to shrink the bulletin down to one folded sheet for that Sunday, feeling like a young filly dancing before the starting gate. Our bulletin had grown to a stapled booklet of three legal size sheets, folded to make 12 pages. I showed Kent my one-sheet sample, and told him that Mark would speak about the huge energy and water savings gained by using less paper—what we handed out on Earth Day would model how conservation would look when applied to our taken-for-granted bulletin. We would project on the wall some of the words that otherwise would be in the bulletin, like the Lord's Prayer, that were familiar to people anyway. The cover art, if shrunk to half size, would allow the order of the service to begin right on the cover.

When I saw Kent winding up, even though he tried to remain open to me, one of his large flock, my dancing feet grew heavy. I stopped and looked at him expectantly. He slowly said it would be okay to do this for this one Sunday.

"Saving resources is good," he said. "But I can't agree to cut the bulletin down after that. The trend, Jean, is actually in the other direction, with growing UCC churches getting their bulletins up to four or five sheets, making sixteen to twenty pages. Visitors don't know the doxology and how we say the Lord's Prayer. We need to reprint these and basic welcoming information each Sunday for new people. I need to grow the church. The bulletin is an important part of helping us grow."

"I understand, Kent," I said, reining in. Disappointment was at least better than no conversation at all, because I had to admit that what we engaged in was a real life argument—listening and weighing, and I had to appreciate that.

Earth Day Sunday arrived. My new Mary Jane flats were too tight—I could feel my smallest nail grating on the next toe. My nerves were buzzing—giving a sermon, even if we didn't call it that, was a first for me, and firsts always set my nerves on fire. I recalled Krista's sympathetic laugh when she learned I was to address the congregation and was nervous about it. She jokingly said it was my turn to maybe feel like being sick. I hadn't known that she was nervous when she spoke so effectively during her turn at the pulpit. She always made me feel good. Now Mark and I sat at the ready in the front row with Wendy. In the back of the Sanctuary, I knew Matt was poised with the projector. I sensed the congregation filling up the pews behind us. I was glad I could just look forward and not meet anyone's eyes just yet.

After the church bell, the opening welcome, and the first hymn came the reading of our chosen scriptures. We chose them to elicit gratitude, and also to nudge thought and action. Mark had chosen Deuteronomy 8:7–10, RSV, and the young liturgist sang out: "For the Lord your God is bringing you into a good land, . . . of fountains and springs, . . . a land of wheat and barley, of vines and fig trees and pomegranates . . ." And then my selection, Job 12:7–10, NRSV: "But ask the animals, and they will teach you; the birds of the air, and they will tell you; ask the plants of the earth, and they will teach you; and the fish of the sea will declare to you . . ." If the congregation can really hear these texts, will they even need Mark's words, or mine? Oh, the passion I felt that year, and oh, the squeeze, compressing all my passion into this one chance, for eight short minutes was what we were allotted. Next, a hymn. I could feel Judy's organ notes alive in me, but I could only murmur, pretending to sing. If I let singing tug on my emotions right then, I'd crack.

The children gathered to sit around Wendy on the floor in front of us. When she had spoken and given out the seedlings, the children exited to church school. Now was the moment for Mark and me. Our turn.

We solemnly climbed the three steps to our waiting high stools in the center of the chancel. We picked up our microphones and settled. Smile and breathe, I reminded myself, and I looked out toward friendly faces and looked up into the balcony, and hard right to the choir. Kent sat to our lower left in the preachers' short row below the pulpit. He didn't look particularly hopeful about our presentation. I wanted to show him that our carefully chosen words were worthy of this displacement, our taking his place on stage, as it were.

I opened with my Holden Village story, Lake Chelan, 1989. "We arrived on a Thursday afternoon unaware that this wasn't a tourist-catering resort, not even a rustic one, but was a bare-bones church camp. Group dormitories, one for men, one for women," and a bathroom building that was off the grid and short of water for flushing. (If it's yellow, let it mellow... I didn't include this from the latrine signage. For lack of time, of course.) My misgivings upon arrival soon worsened into an insult. "We had not been told that Thursday supper was always bread and water. Well, tea as well. I was appalled. Yes, the money these good Lutherans saved on this meal was going to a good cause—the Solidarity Movement in Poland, for justice and self-rule." As I said this, I caught the eyes of Rod MacKenzie, a retired pastor, who smiled broadly at this reference.

Continuing, I recounted, "But, but, I sputtered to Bill, but I'll go to bed hungry!" (I live, like armies are said to, on my belly.) "That's just *great*. They should have warned us so we could bring a sandwich. It doesn't seem fair. And Jenny! We'd brought thirteen-year-old Jennifer all the way from Ohio for a hiking vacation, not bread and water. But Bill and Jenny seemed OK, not upset like I was. The bread arrived, and to my surprise it was *wonderful* bread, hearty with fresh seeds and nuts."

I tried to convey to the congregation that this was not like some bottom-of-the-bulk-foods-bin sunflower seeds that had already aged to rancidity in some silo before reaching the store. "Honey and butter and bread had never tasted so good. I happily ate my fill. And to end the evening, we walked down to the old bowling alley, left over from the days when this was a mining camp. The bowling lanes were still as they had been in those days, that is, without electricity. No electricity meant no automatic pin setter. To need to set the pins by hand tickled Bill and me, stepping into the past like that, and we were instantly primed for fun. Someone got us started. Tall, snake-hipped Jenny stepped up and airmailed her ball halfway down the lane before it clunked to the wood, then to gutter. She tried a few more times, but the frustration got to her and she decided to be a pin setter."

Pin setting goes like this. Your pin setter corrals the pins into a big triangular collar, lifts the collar, and jumps up to sit on a shelf. Soon Bill sent a bowling ball down the lane toward Jenny's dangling feet, and pins flew, and she grinned from her perch. Then she hopped down to set the pins over again. This primitive version of bowling sent us into peals of laughter. In describing this scene for my smiling audience, I began to relax and enjoy the moment, even if one big gesture of mine clunked the microphone. No matter. A moment's startle was all it gave me, and I concluded that our stay in this church camp in this beautiful setting was a sweet time after all, one that we were grateful for, and getting to know our Ohio niece was priceless.

Smoothly, Mark answered me, describing his experience at a Colorado Lutheran camp when he was sixteen and wrestling with his faith. To spend a week away from home was initially the best reason for going. Then against the backdrop of the Sangre de Cristo Mountains he saw how the landscape was a lot like the good land in the Deuteronomy passage. "Minus the figs, pomegranates, and olive trees." At this, a chuckle from our audience. "I stayed out after dark that night for prayer and reflection, and the stars came out, more and more stars, until the sky was a riot of light. I felt so full of life and at the same time so small. I could feel myself a part of Creation, intimately connected to the granite rock, the Ponderosa pine and to all species throughout time in the dance of evolution. A sensing of the grace of God." I smiled to think how similar my beach experience had felt.

From this base, Mark homed in to our Earth Day message: When aware of the gifts of the Creator, Mark said, "the response that makes the most sense to me is to care for the Earth and promote social and ecological justice. I try to do this where I can—from hanging my clothes outside to dry and commuting by bicycle, to engaging my elected representatives on critical environmental issues and challenging myself to avoid the trap of consumerism. This quest is often countercultural and difficult," and perhaps with a touch of motivational flattery, he said he felt blessed to be part of a church community like FCCB that affirms the goodness of Creation and "encourages me to live God's love, justice, and compassion." In this way he tied Earth justice to FCCB's new tagline, ending in dot dot dot to indicate the openness we were invited to hold in our minds and hearts. The unfinished work it all was. To Mark, and to me, the tie between Earth justice and social justice is inseparable. We were trying to move the group. They were listening with wide-awake attention.

I took up the thread. "Now, I was more of a *city* girl. Nature was a scenic backdrop, like a painting. Then when my job ended I found this church and re-started my faith journey. I also slowed down and began to get more from a hike or beach walk. I began to see and feel myself connected in nature, much like you, Mark. This helped me to commit to a 10-week course at WSU Extension called Carbon Masters, learning about climate disruption and pollution impacts facing Whatcom County and beyond." I swiveled hard right to make eye contact with the seated choir that was otherwise out of my sight. I had practiced, and made sure I looked up into the balcony as well at least once or twice.

"What I learned in Carbon Masters frankly overwhelmed me. I keenly felt the depth of our problem. Individual actions are necessary but will not be enough. And technology holds promise, but not enough, nor soon enough. Kent posed a question a few weeks ago in his sermon: 'Amid resource depletion, are we living as though it doesn't matter?' We do need to step it up. But here in this place today," and this is where I put in my own bit of flattery, or encouragement, or cajoling, "I feel encouraged. I believe God has given us enormous reserves of another kind of resource, one that is within ourselves. Within this congregation. For rising to this challenge, together."

We got down to our specific pitches. How can we as a congregation respond? Mark cited our United Church of Christ conference minister—this showed that our message was squarely within our denomination's thinking—who said we can choose anything from the basics to a transformational ministry. Mark's examples showed that our congregation has been involved in each of these approaches at different times, on various issues. Then he tied this concept of choice to describe Green Team's own experiment with less paper in the bulletin. I would have had to take a deep breath, but he started in easily. I looked over at Kent, who was inscrutable behind a Buster Keaton stone face. All Mark said was that, through careful design, today's bulletin used less paper, and we'd printed only a few of the separate sheets of announcements normally stuffed into all copies of the Sunday bulletin. This made sense because many in the membership were now receiving the same announcements by email, another Green Team initiative.

Mark posed the question, Why focus on paper? I knew that he was working for Forest Ethics and wasn't just talking through his hat. Plus he'd researched our paper usage. With Kent holding his breath nearby, Mark only said that producing paper uses massive amounts of energy and water and produces a variety of pollutants. And that trees, especially those in intact forests, play a critical role in sustaining biodiversity, filtering water and removing excess climate-changing carbon from the atmosphere.

With a grace I couldn't have mustered, Mark then backed away from the implication. He averred that whether or not this specific paper usage came to be adopted here, "it might be an example that gets us thinking of ways we can show our gratitude by caring for God's green Earth." I hoped Kent breathed a sigh of relief at our measured, gentle pitch.

Time was growing short. I wrapped up. I told everyone that member Jerry Couchman had done a quiet wonder with our church building, starting with an energy audit. I pitched the Community Energy Challenge for our individual homes, including the local jobs it provides. At the time, many "Good Jobs Now!" signs dotted the town and county, provided by the would-be coal port developers, and I was going to take this rare opportunity of a captive audience to suggest that in going green we can grow good jobs without inviting the coal Goliath to stomp all over our town, though certainly I wasn't going to say it outright. In retrospect, I wonder if I should have said it outright. But I didn't want to damage what we'd done in this few minutes, and I've never wanted to be a lightning rod. Even the brave Jesse Dye of Earth Ministry, a Catholic-led ecumenical Seattle area lobby, whom I mentioned next for her legislative leadership for churches, picked her issues, and ways of speaking about them, carefully.

I closed by pointing out that faith communities can do things that restaurants cannot (charge for a meal and then serve bread and water instead), and church coalitions like Earth Ministry can do what environmental groups sometimes cannot. "Green Team . . . is all of us."

Mark and I stepped down and back into the congregation. I knew I would soon feel exhausted, but at the moment I was relieved and happy to have done what we set out to do. I felt we had connected, even if I didn't know to what extent. The service went on, the hymns, the call for the offering. Certainly there was warmth meeting us, and after the service, a few appreciative greetings, big smiles. One woman told me she'd been inspired to check into the Community Energy Challenge for a home energy audit for her older home.

And then Sundays went back to normal, with only one thing unequivocally having resulted from our effort—the long page of announcements was no longer inserted into each bulletin. Instead, just a few copies were printed to be available on Sunday. A transformative environmental ministry would have to wait, but Green Team had at least enlarged the conversation. We paddle on.

Environmental disappointment was everywhere, including in my Carbon Master classmates. Getting traction in our projects in proportion to the urgency of climate disruption was a steep uphill slog at best. Small steps were celebrated, even while we knew they were small and we were late.

On the other hand, we were still finding out what Minnesotan Timothy Denherder-Thomas said, "I think there's a very important emotional and psychological journey we must go on as we're dealing with something as gigantic as climate change, which is to recognize that we're not going to have a big happy ending to this in any of our lifetimes."[1]

Churches *are* equipped to steel and support us to face what we need to face. But it was going to take time.

1. Denherder-Thomas, "Heart of Climate Justice."

16: Conflict Rears its Head

I signed up for one of the church-wide small group brainstormings—visioning sessions they were called—fodder for the leadership as they plan to propose a plan for the next five years' initiatives. No, that wasn't a typo; a Congregational church undergoes lots of planning-to-plan—discussion, proposals, and getting feedback before big decisions. I chose a group led by Mark Schofield, my Earth Day partner. I was confident in Mark, and curious how it would go.

We met in the Mt. Baker room a few paces past the brushed stainless-steel kitchen. I took my seat at one of the well-upholstered chairs and exchanged pleasantries as people sprinkled themselves in.

The meeting got underway. Across the huge old boardroom-style table from me a man spoke up. In his early forties, Chaz sat with his wife, both vivid of appearance and energy. "We need to make our mark as a congregation," he said with verve. He wanted to use the church basement as homeless housing. Mark wrote the idea in blue on the white board, releasing the sharp smell of the marker.

A fan whirring softly overhead labored to clear the chemical smell. A whiff of coffee was the only other scent in the air. The walls hunkered close at our backs, making the room seem small despite, or because of, the giant conference table. I didn't know the speaker but felt his pilot light was set a little high. I know. I'm not one to talk.

The elderly but keen-eyed Margaret, a woman everyone knew and liked, broke the silence. "Do we know what the Opportunity Council or the Lighthouse Mission would advise? What the needs exactly are?" she asked, naming the city's two major players in social support. Discussion started up, then fell off, inconclusively.

Clint spoke up from the far end of the table where he sat with his quiet wife, Nell. "We've been encouraged from the pulpit to be bold, and I like the boldness of Chaz's idea, but I'd also be concerned about liabilities," he said. Clint was as beige in his camel sport jacket as Chaz was vivid in his dark suit. I was acquainted with Clint, a salt-of-the-earth retired clergyman.

Julie, Margaret's daughter, a woman with a warm sparkle about her, brought the subject down to smaller ambitions. "The diaper ministry could be expanded." Mark wrote it down.

So far we'd been donating disposable diapers. I offered, "Could an expansion get us into encouraging cloth diapers? In order to reduce landfill waste and emissions. Volunteers like me could help young parents get set up to wash diapers rather than depend on disposables."

I looked around at impassive faces, no one reacting. Clunk. Immediately I knew that the best that could be said about my suggestion was I was playing "small ball," like the Mariners did that one year to squeak out runs from piddling slap hits, walks, and steals. Really, Jean, in a visioning meeting? Maybe I'm clueless here. Maybe no low-income parents have a washing machine at home. That the idea would go nowhere would have been fine with me if someone had said something. The folks at the table who focused on immediate human needs, and they seemed the majority in the church, maybe didn't readily make the connection between caring for the planet and caring for people, though the intertwining was in the very air I breathed.

The woman next to me, who'd introduced herself as Amaléa, cleared her throat. I had never seen her before. About seventy in age, neatly and proudly arranged. Quaveringly but with conviction she said, "We should take a stand against coal."

Clint responded, perhaps too quickly. "I'm sorry, but I can't support taking a stand. Nell and I minister to too many families where one is in the hospital, and another has just lost a job in this recession. The coal port means jobs and my compassion for those who are hurting is pretty much what I have to offer."

"I'm sorry, too, but I'm passionate about this," Amaléa said. "It's just too important. And it *is* compassionate." Tension had risen in the room but silence reigned. Amaléa not looking at Clint, but instead across the table, and then forward toward Mark.

Mark listened without speaking. Did that take self-restraint? Young, modest of demeanor despite the asset of Daniel Craig blue eyes, he surely had sympathies for Amaléa's views.

My views squared with Amaléa's as well. I wondered what would help the group. I blurted, "You know, this coal port issue, there are yard signs all over town against it, and signs all over town for it—Good Jobs Now! they say. But, correct me if I'm wrong, this town has not yet had an actual *dialogue* about jobs."

A murmur rippled among the group, exhalations of relief that the tension was drawn away from the two polite combatants. The energy boomeranged to Mark and subsided into the orbit of our main task. But the discord still hung in the air, unacknowledged. I saw in face after face that folks were sweeping it under the rug. I would come to see this as a pattern in this church, one that I could appreciate in the short run, but which reduced my sense of full-trust relationship.

Later at home, I noticed my feet had gone cold, probably from all that sitting, which is not that great for my back. I lay down on the bed, sliding my feet toward the heated buckwheat bag I'd tossed under the lap-sized quilt. My heels caught in one end of the quilt despite my grasp of the other end, so that my toes went ballet-pointed as my legs straightened. I raised my free hand to loosen the quilt, then decided against freeing my feet, the papoose-like binding oddly comfortable, and I sighed with pleasure. Something about anchored heels made my low back relax and soften. Why do I still go to group process meetings? I did that for years in my work, and the introvert in me seldom felt good afterwards. Especially when the group gets stuck. It's no different now that the meetings are voluntary.

Bill and I know something about being stuck. That day described in chapter one, when we were headed for the large boulder? I hadn't been able to get across to Bill what was in front of us. We ran out of time and, yes, we struck that rock. Since it was broad and flattish, and I had been working to evade it, we didn't hit it square on. Our canoe ran up onto the side of the boulder with a sickening, slowing grind and we found ourselves perched, at a precarious leftward tilt, with Bill's end still in the water. Probably only seconds to go before the current would swing the stern into a further tilt and over we would go.

I never got used to dumping in icy water. Even with the benefit of tight-fitted farmer john wet suits, I would flail for a few long seconds to find my breath before I could swim to shore. The neoprene wetsuit and nylon paddling jacket didn't make me feel warm in the water; I was still cold as the icy water invaded the neoprene but warmed just enough so I could breathe and swim, and then swim hard against the current. And we'd never capsized among rocks, in the rapids.

Fortunately, on that day we didn't capsize. My first thought when we ground to an uncertain halt, was Whew. Followed immediately by *We gotta get off of this rock—now!* Bill let me know his thought was the same. Paddlers behind us saw the whole thing and shouted to us they would stop downstream. If we couldn't get free, they'd throw us a rope. But we managed to dislodge ourselves—straining to lean hard right as we had to against the tipping angle, we threw our weight, skooching the canoe forward an inch at a time while shoving our paddles against the boulder. That evening, India Pale Ale never tasted better.

The visioning session had reflected the congregation's stuckness, and we would struggle for some time yet, applying our paddles and skooching our weight this way and that, but we would in time find our way off that boulder.

17: A Just Peace

G reen Team was faltering, chugging to a halt. It had been a pretty decent run. As a last gasp, one of our group, Dorothy S., who was also an alum of Carbon Masters with me, arranged for the church to begin composting our coffee hour food scraps and paper napkins. It quickly became normal to scrape plates into the bin brightly tagged for the local compost pick-up program. Visitors staying for refreshments after memorial services also caught on to the drill.

Dorothy's attention was now taken up with her daughter's move to Alaska. Rob had changed to a job with an unstable schedule and couldn't lead meetings. Tony moved away. So did Sherry, to the sailing life. And so it went.

Where would I plug in next? I started going to the meetings of the Just Peace committee, hoping for others looking for environmental projects that would grab the hearts of a justice-oriented congregation better than simple green actions had done. The national UCC office had renewed a social justice push by offering its member congregations a model declaration in support of "A Just Peace." Meaning, of course, more than the absence of war or active conflict alone.

I led an adult forum before worship one Sunday, to provide an orientation to environmental justice. I talked about estimates of 200 million climate refugees by 2050, and how we've already seen refugees created by climate change within our borders—in 2005 tribal members of the Biloxi-Chitim-acha-Choctaw and Houma Nation had their homes washed away and the U.S. Department of Housing and Urban Development provided the funds to move them. The attendance at that early hour of 8:30 was encouraging. My friend Helen was at my side and I met new church-goers, too.

The small Just Peace committee had put on a picnic the previous year at a time I couldn't go. They were going to have environmental protest performer Dana Lyons at the picnic. That really pricked up my ears. Lyons became famous for his hilarious 1996 song, "Cows with Guns," and he'd kept adding to his repertoire, traveling widely—rural Australia was among his appearances in between stints here, including in the monthly radio show put on by local independent bookstore Village Books. We'd sung "Cows" at an annual Group Health employee picnic when the song was already a few years old, and it didn't cross my mind there'd be controversy about Lyons at FCCB. But the Just Peace picnic planners were asked not to invite him—if he did a song about the coal port it might offend some folks. That was the reasoning one of them recalled hearing at the time.

That's when I first became aware of divisions in FCCB—not simply a stray disagreement like between Clint and Amaléa. Divisions that weren't minor, that weren't ephemeral. Why should that surprise me? Divisions, while muted by wonderful fellow-feeling, simply mirrored different ways of seeing things in the larger society, even though FCCB skewed left. At least when expressed, our differences are gently put, lacking in the partisan glee or the desire to hurt or shock that pervades our larger world. At that time, Church Council, those empowered to speak for the whole, seemed not to want to take on environmental fights. Maybe they thought they were being neutral and avoiding conflict by staying out of an issue—the local issue of the day was misleadingly framed by industry as jobs versus the environment. If you were alert, that meant temporary coal port construction jobs vs. permanent damage and very few subsequent permanent jobs. I hate fighting as much as the next person, but conflicting viewpoints need to be aired. And I wonder how often neutrality is only illusory. In this case, business as usual would be letting industry dictate to communities and governments, and send the public the bill for the inevitable cleanup. All while pushing Native and white fishers under the bus. Neutrality was not truly available.

I used to rack my mind with questions about how I could possibly withhold judgment of others' mental landscapes. Not to dutifully be a better Christian, but because I'd become convinced it would be good for my happiness. Now I ponder if it is a matter of the eye—what people can see or not see. Some of us are near-sighted and some are far-sighted, and bless us, I know we need both kinds of eyes, both kinds of people. On a good day, that's what I know. And on a practical level, I've had to acknowledge that for any given action it helps if the moment is ripe. A church must rest from time to time, and concentrate on nurturance. Fortunately, others in the wider community had made coal resistance a major, extended effort, most notably the Lummi Nation. More on this in the next chapter.

The council was much more on board with the social justice initiative, A Just Peace, and gave the approval to declare our church A Just Peace church. The committee had a beautiful logo and banner made, and put on a celebration in 2013 for the Just Peace declaration, taking over the Narthex one Sunday with tables decorated with greenery that I remember contributing from the abundance of cedars in our home's adjoining woodlot.

As a member of the committee, I also grabbed my opportunity to commandeer some of the table space for literature highlighting the justice issues in the environmental movement—to broaden the topic. One item I displayed was about Monsanto. My friend Lynn Dager came by, looked down at my display and smiled.

"My late husband knew long ago that Monsanto was a problem. He was an engineer working for General Electric in the 1950s, working next door to a Monsanto plant. Monsanto was making Accent, a food flavor enhancer—you may recall, it's mostly MSG. But the fumes from their plant made the G.E. employees sick. What you are doing is good, Jean. I feel like I was born too soon. Now I'm too old to help with these issues."

I wasn't so sure she was really too old to be a part of a movement, but her support buoyed me. And in small ways like this, I kept at my climate work. Another minor project was collecting plastic bags from interested parties at church every few months. The local curbside recycling did not take them, and I took bundles of them in Bill's old truck to the drop-off bins at the garbage company's office for $5.00. It was something, at least while we still thought plastics were readily recyclable into new products, before China brought us up short by ending their program. Better to re-use or refuse, anyway, if possible, and we have since moved in that better direction.

Was A Just Peace going to stall, stopping at pretty words? Perhaps not. I had heard in my pre-joining inquirers' class many of the highlights of UCC doings and milestones—indeed, what I learned had stoked my optimism about church activism. Now I needed a booster shot of perspective in order to bolster my patience. I returned to my notes taken in FCCB's inquirer's class, and leafed through "Short Course in the History of the United Church of Christ" from the Education and Mission Section of their web site, ucc.org.

The Congregationalists, together with the sister churches making up the UCC, brought a long and rich history. My posture straightened just from seeing some of the "firsts." The first school for the deaf, which became Gallaudet, in New York, in 1817. The first integrated anti-slavery society was formed in 1846 in the wake of the Amistad case, with multiracial leadership—that was the key new thing our ancestral church leaders required, that the very leadership be integrated. The first woman pastor to receive a calling was Antoinette Brown. She finished her studies at Oberlin but they refused to grant her degree, and it took her three years to find a church that would call her, but finally the Congregational church of Butler, New York, did so in 1853, and she was ordained there. If I'm to be accurate, she wasn't the first woman minister in a Christian church, but the first in modern times, because, as I mentioned earlier, women's roles were pretty equal to men's at the *start* of the Christian church.

The new UCC's head of communications didn't sit behind a desk—he was the Indiana Jones of 1960s administrators. According to the 2015 obituary for the Reverend Everett Parker by Los Angeles Times writer David Colker, Parker made a crusade against a radio station bent on suppressing news about the growing Civil Rights movement. It began with a 1963 call from Martin Luther King, Jr. asking the UCC to intervene on the evident news blackout, particularly blatant at a Jackson, Mississippi cable TV station. They had a wrong-headed idea of what "to serve the public interest" meant, to put it mildly. Parker first went to the FCC. No help there. He had "no standing" to call for a hearing. Then, having been warned how to stay safe, he "quietly established a viewing post in the home of a Jackson family sympathetic to his cause. He trained a group of 22 local citizens in how to carefully monitor and note what the station was showing. But he was careful not to learn their names," so that when it came time for him to testify, they couldn't be identified. The FCC still renewed the station's license. "The matter went back and forth in court until 1969, when the U.S. Court of Appeals sided with Parker, stripping the owners of the license."[1]

In another milestone, the first openly gay man to be ordained in any Protestant denomination was William R. Johnson, ordained in 1972 by a UCC church. The UCC General Synod supported Marriage Equality by resolution in 2005. How does such a resolution work, exactly, if this church is not hierarchical? This is how it was explained to me in the inquirers' class: Resolutions by the General Synod may be adopted by a congregation or not as they choose. Individual Congregational churches are not even required to join the UCC. They can remain separate under the Congregational name, and when the UCC was formed, a few did so.

I wasn't sure that this historical perspective would help my patience about activism now, but it didn't hurt to feel pride in the ancestry of one's wider family.

A last history note, just to make me smile: I found that the UCC tagline, "God is Still Speaking," was inspired by Gracie Allen of the classic comedy duo Burns and Allen, when she said, "Never place a period where God has placed a comma." TV commercials the UCC created in the early 2000s used humor, with ejector seats in the pews kicking out one after another "different" attendee in some unnamed church, to make a point of contrast with UCC inclusiveness. The TV networks didn't find these commercials amusing. They refused to air the spots, according to the UCC's "Short Course," so the UCC couldn't pay to get their commercials aired, but they had the last laugh when the TV news played the spots over and over in reporting on the controversy. Remember those days, when news was separated from other network decision-making?

1. Colker, "Rev. Everett Parker."

18: Joining Hands with Lummi Nation

Our church had been unable to make a resolution siding with the Lummi on the coal port issue, but there had to be an action some of us could take. And, interestingly, it was the church that provided me a great opportunity. But first, another coal port flop, this one on the jobs issue. In short, Amaléa and I wanted to create a community dialogue about what it might take to better support local businesses, rather than national chains and mega businesses. We weren't able to get any such thing going at church or in the community. Even a slogan like "Jobs with Justice" meant something different to us than it meant to the labor union whose meeting she and I attended looking for an avenue. To them at that time, the focus was fair wages, and union access to all the jobs—the *kinds* of jobs were less important. Build a coal port; clean up after an oil spill; all, you know, jobs.

Early the next year, 2013, and this is where the great opportunity comes in, Mark G., a sunny, ruddy-faced man closely involved with church leadership, suggested another avenue for Amaléa and me to pursue. An interfaith group was forming, hosted by Bellingham Unitarian Fellowship. The new group was forming to support the Lummi, who were trying to get their treaty rights respected and not end up with a giant coal port next to their fishing grounds at Cherry Point, trampling lands with sacred value in the process. This would mean stepping into a world quite foreign to me.

Mere inklings were all I'd ever had of the potential cooperation between whites and Native Americans. Certainly, an appreciation and even borrowing from indigenous peoples was a cultural current I'd been picking up. Even in church. We'd had a prayer one Sunday that we read in unison, and it was credited as coming from "Polished Arrows: Service Prayers," written by Marilyn K. Levine, UCC pastor on the Fort Berthold Indian Reservation in North Dakota.

I loved its ending—I loved the purpose it imputes to Jesus' life, *to show us who we are*. But for actual knowledge of Native Americans, the renowned advocate for the environment David Suzuki was perhaps the first messenger I truly heard. In the previous May, 2012, using the prerogative of a retiree to go to a noon lecture, I walked up Indian Street (now happily renamed Billy Frank, Jr. Street in honor of the Nisqually tribal fishing rights activist) to the university to hear Mr. Suzuki speak. I waited for the doors to open as the line lengthened behind me, and chatted with people about what brought them. Nice folks, and I felt a sense of community, suggesting that I needed to get out more. Having arrived early, I got a second row seat and was excited to be up close to the man himself as he waited in the front row in a cranberry-red silk shirt. He had company with him and I did not interrupt.

When he took the podium, I was struck by the first thing he said. He thanked the Native Americans he saw. On the heels of that, he said he'd come to speak as an elder. I wondered: Do they have that concept in his native Japan, the elder as Native Americans have constructed elder? I listened for why, either way, this was important to him.

He told of his visits to First Nations villages in British Columbia, especially in what used to be known as the Queen Charlotte Islands, now on the map as Haida Gwaii. He said that we've framed the environmental protection problem all wrong. In the 1970s he didn't understand at first how a big chunk of the Haida people managed to spurn the logging jobs. This is what whites do to each other as well as to people of color all the time: go to an economically depressed area with an offer they can't refuse. But the Haida did refuse. One man told Suzuki, "We Haida don't end at our skin . . . we're connected to the land." Being absorbed into the dominant ways "would mean we'll then be like everyone else." Oh! So, in that North Dakota prayer that said Jesus showed us who we are, that was an identity statement. Only, both of these expressed identity of a much deeper kind than the garden variety social and cultural identity we're all familiar with.

Northwesterner, tree-hugger, Rotarian, etc. I wanted to absorb that for a bit, not let that moment just flit by.

Yet here came more: Haida identity being so connected with nature, "who we are would go away." Who we are would *go away*. This was haunting.

Suzuki expanded the thought in ways that helped his message sink in and not seem so strange, or so alien from typical American frameworks about our individual selves and where the edges are. The oxygen you breathe is exhaled and goes into me, he said, and then back into you. Maybe the same oxygen molecules that Jesus breathed have been breathed by you. There is no line between the air and us. Same for water, and earth.

Then he addressed all the older people present: "Get the hell off the golf course and get on to the most important work of your life!" How did he know when he prepared his lecture that there would be more retirees in the audience that day than students? I looked behind me and saw that my fellow oldsters liked this exhortation. Somehow these didn't look like golf fanatics, but it made a good rallying cry, anyway. His challenge to the educated also struck home: "It's not higher education unless it's put to higher purposes."

Invigorated by this time with David Suzuki, I went to the first interfaith meeting. At one of the round banquet tables in the daylight basement at Bellingham Unitarian Fellowship (BUF) were a Buddhist, a Catholic, a retired Lutheran minister, a Methodist minister who is pastor of a church on the Nooksack Native reservation, three of us from FCCB, and two Unitarians. One of us from FCCB was Wendy Scherrer, who had given out the cedar trees to the children on Earth Day. She had formerly headed up the local salmon recovery organization known as NSEA, the Nooksack Salmon Enhancement Association, and had established close working relationships with the Lummi Business Council and other Lummi leaders. Deb Cruz and the other Unitarian, Beth Brownfield, likewise had ties with members of the Lummi tribe, and were deeply committed to channels of communication and friendship with them. Our new interfaith group's animating purpose: If we could show an equivalence between places we non-Natives revered and places Native peoples held as sacred ground and sacred waters, their rights could come out from under whites' mental rug, and hopefully find support.

Deb briefed us on the recent stage play that the Lummi had created, performed, and filmed to expose the wider community to the background of losses their tribe had suffered. The play also made palpable the sheer weight of 10,000 years during which the land and fisheries had a high and unchanging value to the tribe. We on the committee let our church-es know about the next performance, and Shantel from our Just Peace committee attended and was deeply moved. Deb, with her experience in graphic art, laid out a color brochure about sacred ground in faith tradi-tions all over the world. The Lummi House of Tears Carvers wanted to take this brochure with them on an upcoming totem pole journey, and so we hustled to get it ready in time. Out of the group discussion, the Lu-theran minister also drafted a Statement of Solidarity, and the group made some adjustments, changing language that wasn't yet a good fit with all of the traditions we represented. And we had it! The brochure was beautiful, and so was the Statement of Solidarity.

Soon we were collecting solidarity signatures in our respective churches and communities. Amaléa and I set up a table in the Narthex for three Sunday mornings. The two of us had developed a handout, and I also had a photo album of Bill's and my recent trip to Gettysburg. Work-ing with the Lummi view of sacred ground made stark how commodified most U.S. places had become. And so, by being tuned to it, I'm quite sure I found at Gettysburg a deeper gut experience than if I'd not been on this committee—and if I'd not been a regular in church. I shot quite a few photos while there, guided by my feelings.

Most of the people who stopped at our table in the Narthex signed the Statement of Solidarity, though some gave us a wide berth. We col-lected forty signatures total. That's out of some 200 attending on any given Sunday. Now, on any Sunday of the year many things vie for attention in this busy church. Still, forty signatures was modest, and indicated at least ambivalence to the issue. A lack of mention from the pulpit despite my thrusting a brief announcement into Kent's hand no doubt sent a signal as well. But some delightful encouragement came our way. Julie G., for one, who'd been in the visioning workshop I'd attended. Always a positive influ-ence, this time she was very specific.

"Where do I sign?" she said. "I'm glad of this opportunity. I've never forgotten the support that the Lummi provided for us San Juan Islands resi-dents when we had an environmental battle to fight."

Even where people saw things differently, I appreciated a forthright exchange whenever I could find it. "Can we have both the coal port and Lummi sacred ground protection?" That was a soft, concerned question from Palmer.

"It seems to be one or the other, Palmer," I said.

"Then I'm afraid I can't sign."

I nodded. I was still there with him in friendship.

I sent our forty signatures on our Statement of Solidarity to our U. S. Senator, Maria Cantwell, who sat on oversight committees for both the Army Corps of Engineers and the Bureau of Indian Affairs. My letter was of course careful to be clear that I wasn't speaking for the church as a whole. I'd hoped for more, of course I had. More signatures and an all-church resolution would have been wonderful to present to Sen. Cantwell. It wasn't to be, not without the support of the council and Kent. Still, I'd had a wonderful experience in the interfaith task group that I wouldn't have had without my membership in FCCB. That a church could be capable of opening really cool doors hadn't occurred to me when I joined. The Lummi House of Tears Carvers received copies of the FCCB signatures, and the signatures and even official church statements from other faith communities, which added up to a lot of support. Overall, a happy moment in time.

It wasn't long before Amaléa, disappointed that First Congregational wasn't doing more, left FCCB and found a project in town to which she could devote herself. Krista H. had left as well, a bit disappointed and also needing to attend to family concerns, and that caused me sadness. I talk with her occasionally and still miss her at church.

The various citizen groups that mounted a huge effort under the umbrella of the Power Past Coal campaign sacrificed many volunteer hours to stave off an expanded coal port on our waterfront. But it was clear that the Lummi did the most and were the most crucial. They had rights that could not be steamrolled over, *if* recognized officially and publicly. Which was no sure thing, to put it mildly. They showed a level of unified leadership that the rest of us could only admire. Ultimately, the community as a whole won some important battles and at least we won't have giant piles of coal in the open, dusting us each time the well-known wind of Ferndale, a town a few miles north, blows. The small shipping port will not be expanded, though there were several more runs at it, followed by promotion of an oil pipeline plan to the same seaport area, still a threat years later.

I now saw the steadfast activism of the Lummi people as part of a much wider resurgence. It almost seems like an indigenous peoples' resurgence has been in the air, maybe all over the world. Indigenous people have been coming forward, reaching out to the rest of us with gifts from which restorative relationships can develop. I've felt an energy, a comet I wanted to latch onto. This rising is not just about the coal terminal, although that and issues like it elsewhere have forced it to wide recognition. It's like the time has come, grossly belated but inexorable, when the general populace finds they can look fully and honestly at North American Native peoples. And respond to them as the brothers and sisters white people have been blind to, and worse.

Before this resurgence, too many of us seemed surprised, even in this new century, that Native peoples are still around as cohesive cultures and tribes or bands and businesses, as well as individually, with modern-day stories, and music. In blues-rock and other popular music, I love that they have reclaimed iconic performances and authorship achieved while they were constrained to submerge their Native identities. Just for two, Robbie Robertson of The Band, and before him, Link Wray. "Rumble," the Link Wray & the Raymen instrumental, made blues-rock history in 1958, with its power chords and undulating pulse. I first heard it some years later as covered by The Ventures and felt the gut-buzz of it. But when I finally saw video of a performance by Wray, what he shook from his guitar went through me like I was a tuning fork; I would have followed him anywhere. The Klan had sent Wray's family into hiding more than once in his young life in the 1930s and it wasn't until 1971 that he went public with his Indian identity. That is wrenching to know, and to realize that the Klan and its movement of intimidation damaged all of us when they suppressed the free expression, suppressed the thriving, of indigenous people for all those decades. The Klan was too successful in helping create the false impression that Natives were somehow bygone as peoples and cultures. Yet their harm is undone, bit by bit, year by year. The declaration in "Rumble" resonates with each generation of American young people still.

I went to a totem pole blessing ceremony out at Cherry Point, near the site the coal proponents lusted for. I needed directions and GPS to find the spot on Lummi land. We left our cars strung out for a half-mile along the narrow approach road. A trickle of walkers became a large gathering on the skinny beach, where a heavy-duty flatbed truck bore the prostrate form of a colorful totem pole. Lummi elder and master carver Jewell James with his wife Ramona James stood on the flatbed in front of the impressive girth of the totem pole. Visiting dignitaries joined them, including representatives from the First Nations group from British Columbia who would be receiving this gift after its travels. All spoke in turn, eloquently, solemnly. The crowd was rapt, as I was. But it was Jewell and Ramona James who made me feel like the Lummi were sharing their elders with us white folk. Not exhorting us, nor merely tolerating us, nor even accepting us only as allies, but sharing their souls. To be sure, there might have been an element of showmanship; that is certainly true of most of our own pastors and not a bad thing. I mean to evoke presentation skills, not Barnum and Bailey. Any showmanship was in service of connecting. Certainly I was moved and felt reinforced in my own efforts within my church. This was a resonance that would return several times, including on a carpool trip with Unitarian Beth Brownfield to Seattle's St. Mark's Episcopal Cathedral for another totem pole blessing and dedication. That one included on the dais FCCB's own area conference minister, who also briefly spoke, making me proud.

Beth also told me about a symposium. I went to it, a meaty and friendly educational event that furthered my understanding of my Lummi neighbors and of the history of governmental and white roadblocks—blocks erected against fairness, understanding, and friendship between peoples. Injustice that was sobering, but the saga provided me a deeper understanding. Deeper, in that a fuller picture of human failings and historical patterns invites more overall compassion than does the shortcut word, racism, with that word's emphasis on blame, individual shame, and of course, division. Educational events like this, together with the mainstream media increasingly providing news about Native Americans, all feel part and parcel of this river of life I'm paddling. One more culverted stream was opened to daylight; one more current freshened the river.

When the Lummi took their turn hosting the annual Coast Salish tribes canoe journey events, my sister Julie and I went to the youth canoe races. What beautiful wooden canoes; we examined three of them resting on the pebbled saltwater shore between races, their varnish gleaming butterscotch in the sun.

After the heinous attack on the New York Trade Center in 2001, the Lummi House of Tears Carvers made a totem pole to offer for healing. That early totem pole journey across the country must have seemed quixotic to most Americans, if they were even aware of the ceremonial trip. After much talk about "the terrorists" and an invasion of Iraq, Americans couldn't deny we were uneasy about things. As we Americans sought happiness beyond what a trip to the mall could provide (remember President Bush's urgings to just go shopping), many turned to the self-help sections of bookstores searching for new messages. But more than fifteen years on, that totem pole stands in the children's garden at the memorial site, its message unfaddish and unfaded.

19: Confessing a Dislike for America's Favorite Hymn

After the spiritual resonance I felt in my encounters with the Lummi, it seems penny-ante to carp about the words in one hymn. Nevertheless, I have never liked America's most popular hymn. I'm just guessing it's the most popular, but that's my final answer, Regis. From Judy Collins' 1960s version to hymn-singing at funerals, "Amazing Grace" is everywhere. I've no quarrel with "I was blind, but now I see." It is a lovely line. But why require me to declare myself a wretch? Why, as a woman in this culture that has debased women more often than it has invited equal participation, do I need to sing self-abasement? The wretch part, and the dirge-like cadence of so many renditions, have set my teeth on edge. Unless the song is sung by Judy Collins, of course.

My attitude started shifting in 2016 when we sang "Amazing Grace" at the memorial service for a beloved woman in our congregation, by her own prior request. This time I noticed that our hymnal had new information for me: Stanzas 1–4 date all the way to 1779. Our hymnal calls these stanzas autobiographical, by one John Newton. He was a penitent slave trader! This does alter my view of the hymn. I can celebrate the author's new life that he gained by repentance. And though I have never been a slave trader, I can acknowledge my long-insulated ignorance of the oppression of Black Americans, Native Americans, and others, the oppression I have no doubt, really no doubt, benefited from, however indirectly and unwittingly, given the tilt of our economic and legal environment. I'm glad for the falling away of my individual ignorance, even if I don't call myself a wretch. That memorial service honored Ellen D., who often said to her own family, "Give one another the benefit of the doubt." So "Amazing Grace" works better for me now that I give it the same benefit.

Actually, while in pop culture, as if we are nothing but an audience to be entertained, we have worn out the word *amazing*, we neglect the word grace. Grace is such a terrific cross-over idea—if we let it, it bathes and refreshes us whether we consider it in secular or in religious modes. It soaks our aches, it opens our pores; it is almost as ancient as water itself. Modern usage traces to Old English, and to Latin before that. A cousin word is found in Sanskrit. I like that it is both verb and noun, and that "gracing" something confers dignity or honor on it. Graceful movement reveals ease and suppleness. Its usage is relaxation itself: unmerited assistance given, a "grace period," a disposition to kindness, courtesy or clemency. Grace allows regeneration to occur. We all need that; individually, and to keep and repair our interpersonal, societal bonds. When I think how I've taken for granted the grace that my mother showered on my childhood, I can begin, just begin, to gawp at what children face who aren't so showered.

In religion, divine grace can regenerate us so that we can share grace outward. Ellen would agree, I'm sure. The happiness in that little word is, well, amazing.

And after singing about grace, we need to work to do justice, and to repair and restore right relationships. Of all kinds. Then God's grace comes from our many human hands. Like the grace of the Lummi totem pole in the New York children's garden, a sentinel example to us all.

20: Lost in Translation

Why do Christians, at least outside of scholarly circles, not talk more often about the problem of translation? If we did, we might be more humble and uncertain about the meanings of various Bible passages. I suspect we fear a shake-up, or at least an argument about whether The Word is set in stone or not. But we don't fear textual research on the secular side of things, do we?

I came across a humble example about cooking asparagus. Cooks know that the stems take longer to get done than the tender tips (the trend of baby asparagus notwithstanding). So there's a fact to set anchor on. Somewhere around the first century, imperial Romans compiled a cookbook, *Apicus De Re Coquinaria*. Many of the recipes, according to an article in *The Shepherd* by Ari Levaux, were written in vulgar (informal) Latin, which complicated the translation of this cookbook, as scholars looked at "rursum in calidam" and could only understand the last part, "in boiling water." But if you follow only what you can understand, you ruin the asparagus, overcooking the tops and turning them to mush, and surely they knew that. One translator finally cracked the problem in 1936. "Rursum" in this case meant "backwards," and backwards meant stems down.

I didn't know before rediscovering church, but Bible translation is no small thing. I found a biggie posted on ProgressiveChristianity.org: "The phrase 'will live forever' found in . . . the NRSV (New Revised Standard Version) is a distortion of the Greek text 'will live into the age,' meaning the new age of the kingdom of God, not an eternal life in heaven. Likewise, the phrase 'eternal life' is the 'life of the new age' in Greek. Unfortunately, we are often misled by translators with a theological agenda."[1] Perhaps this interpretation is subject to argument, and that's okay. However, it is important to me to see such challenges made.

Getting down to it, what about names for God? Now, I am charmed by casual speech, like one friend's exclamations of "Lordy!" At the same time, in church, "Lord" has always struck me, with my twenty-first century frame of reference, as needlessly frozen in medieval and pre-medieval times. I picture all the bowing and scraping in historical stories presided over by kings. Is that kind of obeisance necessary if we are children of God? Shouldn't we then be knights and ladies, or even dukes and duchesses, that serfs and other vassals look up to and fear to trigger our wrath? Ah, the limits of metaphor. In my anti-authoritarian grudge-holding I was sure the source of "Lord" had to be in the early books in the Bible. But the more you look, the more the usage resolves into an accident of history, not coming from Jewish scribes, let alone "inerrant" scripture. It came from a translation.

I first had to know something about the Jewish view of the divine. This view is implied by references to God as YHWH, letters that can't be and were not meant to be pronounced. So I thought that in Judaism the name of God is too sacred to be uttered. My friend Rabbi Mark Glickman, who is the author of *Sacred Treasure—the Cairo Genizah,* and *Stolen Words: The Nazi Plunder of Jewish Books,* wrote me to fill out and adjust my understanding. He said, "In Jewish tradition, the name of God was so sacred that it was only uttered by one person, once a year—that was when the High Priest entered the Holy of Holies on the Jewish Day of Atonement and addressed God by this ineffable name." Rabbi Glickman, who is Reform, by the way, not ultra-orthodox, also suggested to me a play, "The Dybbuk" by S. An-Ski. A passage in that play, or in Glickman's paraphrasing, ends with this beauty: "Every spot where a person stands and looks toward heaven is a holy of holies. Every day of one's life is a Day of Atonement and every person is a high priest, and every word that a person utters in holiness and purity is the Name of God."

Count on thinkers to never leave a mystery alone. My friend also said many theories try to suggest a pronunciation YHWH. His favorite is

---

1. Struckmeyer, "Words of the Eucharist," para 10.

that the V was actually a letter once pronounced as something between a V and a W, so YHWH was really the sound of breath. Breath, which is much like saying that God is life.

The term Lord was used in secular contexts by both Romans and Christians in the first century. And so it transferred into the Christian scriptures. History is so messy. I'm never going to know the dynamic play-by-play whereby the emperor was addressed as Lord, and who co-opted what as the new Jesus religion began. But I'm satisfied that Lord is secular-cultural in origin and not a sacred term. Bible translators of the Hebrew scriptures substituted Lord for YHWH. As a trivia note, the translators of the texts for the New King James Version were meticulous enough that each instance where YHWH was translated as Lord it was shown stylized in small caps, LORD. Late in this quest I had further help from our pastor, Sharon. In modern Jewish discussion you find the term HaShem, she said, which translates as "The Name." I share her enthusiasm: "How cool is that?" So now when I see the word "Lord" I can smile to recall all that.

Not long after hearing this from Sharon, I spoke again with Jamie, the non-church-going friend who observed that she and I come at Biblical words differently. We sat at a window table in a 1950s-era cafe sipping hot tea on a chilly day. She was encouraging of my pursuits, but as I heard her talk about the tangible, full-fleshed writing she was working on, I began to think that my attention to words and concepts may be just fussy, something that no one else cares about. So I was floored soon after by another writer friend who is a member in a mainline, at least semi-modern, church. At our writers association happy hour we share short readings. Alys opened her eyes wide as I read my bit which casually refers to unfolding my yoga mat in the Barlow Room at Timberline Lodge. When the meeting ended, she scrambled through the obstacles of chairs and the milling crowd to get to me. Knowing that I am a churchgoer, she expressed surprise, eyebrows raised questioningly, at my mention of yoga. Nonplussed, unable to think what in the world she was talking about, I asked her to explain.

"Yoga." she said. "My church won't say the word."

"Why not?" I asked, incredulous.

"Because it would be introducing Buddhist teaching into Christian teaching. Like, we actually did a meditation in church, ended by the little bell, but they wouldn't call it meditation. Didn't use that word."

She seemed to be reacting like Lynn and I did that Sunday when surprise questions were posed of the pastors: Can you *say* that? Alys wasn't scandalized; she just had trouble reconciling this disclosure. In the moment I think I protested that yoga to many is just an exercise routine, and that yoga, or even overtly borrowing from Buddhist thought is not an issue at my church. I didn't tell her we have a church member teaching a yoga class in the church basement every Wednesday. If simple, innocent yoga is such an issue, I wonder what she'd think of the guest preacher we had one Sunday who identified as both Muslim and Christian.

Staying humbly open-minded and not letting our Christian discipline become fetters on our thinking is the key to my being in church. That's what my exploration of words and concepts means to me. It's the *only* way I can be in church. Words can unlock doors as easily as they can lock them. I am also done with compartmentalizing myself to belong to something essentially separate from the world outside its walls. I have to be of a piece. What's more, how can we see ourselves as brothers and sisters with Buddhists while fearing contamination? Is Christianity so fragile, or are parishioners so little trusted?

21: Of Goldilocks, Kitchen Timers, and Blood Sacrifice

I was about to start this chapter with a complaint. Just when I thought I had smooth going as far as the eye could see, my canoe whooshed right into the tangled branches of an ecclesiastical tree lying in the river in front of me, halting my progress. Language about blood sacrifice came back into our communion ritual. Oh, no, not that! It's funny coming right after I ended the last chapter saying "Is Christianity so fragile?" How much like Goldilocks do I want to be, looking for the bowl of oatmeal that's not too hot and not too cold, but just right?

When our kitchen timer quit on us, erupting into cheeps, squawks, and screeches before settling into a silence that a new battery could not budge, Bill set out for a new one. I assumed he would shop carefully and bring home the one best timer, a shining pleasure to use, easy to set, easy to read, easy to hear. Why I would assume this after decades knowing Bill is another question. He's as free-spending as I am frugal. Here's what he brought home: four timers. One old-fashioned, hand-crank, loud ticking, school-bell blaring timer. Fine, that can be his, with his penchant for antiques. One small, big-button timer of OK loudness but lacking an "hour" button. That's a real deficit in a timer. One had a magnet to stick it on the fridge, with a wire bale jutting out to tilt the face upward. So it doesn't stay attached when you touch a button, and you must pick it up off the floor. Maybe gather up the battery and little door and put it back together. When instead you set it on the counter it skitters away as your fingers chase it around. No. One timer he bought was just right for me, and that's the one I use.

Despite my desire to have a generous perspective on the old and new, some of the old bits still irked me every bit as much as I thought they would before I started this church thing. Not the actual rituals, but the words that sometimes went with them. Communion is a ritual that I find moving, as I've said. But I got used to pastors Scott and Kent saying the cup was a new covenant, and I thought that was the official Congregational way of speaking, so when another said the blood thing, blood shed to forgive your sins, I was dismayed. It felt like going backward in time. Now, I will say that sharing part of Christ in Communion, metaphorical blood and body in remembrance can be beautiful, until the added words "shed for you." Those words, and they are in the Bible, are taken to be about atonement, about Jesus as a sacrifice before God for everyone's sins. Even, in some passages, God is *requiring* that kind of substitutional atonement (Hebrews 7:27, Romans 5:9). I checked several translations of these two passages, hoping to find one that didn't have that meaning. Please bear with me here—I promise to wrap this part up quickly. Marcus J. Borg says that sacrifices in the older books of the Bible, the Hebrew texts, were never about substitution—as in a sacrificial lamb substituting for a person's sins. Rather, sacrifices in those times were "to make something sacred by offering it up to God." He describes how "often within Judaism, the animal was cooked and then eaten by those offering the sacrifice, symbolically creating a meal with God, communion with God, . . . Gift and meal often go together in sacrifice."[1]

I can only conclude that we have layered some barnacles onto the notion of sacrifice, changing the meaning to suit a theological agenda that we don't need now, if we ever did. I can hold to my heart an obvious meaning of Jesus' death: He died because established powers were threatened by his teachings, and he held fast for us, even though it cost him his life. This concern about differing interpretations was no longer just about my personal preferences. I was becoming attached enough to this church that I wanted other progressive types like me to feel welcomed here, and I felt, rightly or

1. Borg, *Speaking Christian*, 102.

wrongly, that progressive Christianity's ability to draw modern people can't go so well with the old Christian saws.

I wanted the faith I followed to be cleanly apart from the too-pervasive centuries of patriarchal honor and duty killings in fiction and in reality—reaching back to the Greek tragedies (the story of Agamemnon's sacrificing Iphigenia), and to the lore about the ancient Aztecs, and, I shudder to think, in pockets of today's world. If patriarchal violence had to be in any way part of my modern faith, that would be more than just a crack in my paddle. I like knowing that the ancestors of the Jewish people made a break, in the oldest books of the Old Testament, from the common world view and sacrifice practices all around them. Christians and everyone owe a debt to the ancient people of Abraham that they felt called to become the Israelites, a people devoted to a loving God.

As the earliest writer in the New Testament, the hugely influential Apostle Paul may have kicked off the blood derby. Paul wrote his first letter to the community at Corinth in Greece around the year 54 CE, a little over 20 years after the death of Jesus, even before the gospels were written. As I gathered from Kurt Struckmeyer, Paul shared the Eucharistic tradition (Communion) he had learned from members of a Hellenistic Christ cult in Damascus, Syria. When he, or the Pauline author, wrote, "This cup is the new covenant in my blood," 1 Corinthians 11:25 NRSV, he stopped there. Decades later, the gospel of Matthew added, "which is poured out for many for the forgiveness of sins." (Matthew 26:28 RSV and NRSV). And later got more pointed still in other books of the New Testament, as mentioned above.

References to salvation, when they came up, also set me to brooding. This is a concept connected to sacrifice but also distinct from it. FCCB doesn't preach on salvation or make altar calls, but there are references in hymn and scripture. I tried to think it away. Would I not expect marketing to have been operating in ancient times basically the same as now? When the New Testament was being put together, starting maybe 70 years after Jesus' death, and for two to three centuries after Jesus, the fledgling church must have had leaders who recognized a need to grow. And amid those dangerous times following the burning of the Temple, they came up with a great deal. I am sorry to impute crassness to what could have been a result of much honest argument and factional sparring over time. But maybe I'm not wrong. Dr. Paul C. Dilley of the University of Iowa, when interviewed in 2018, said there had been a profusion of texts and gospels before the New

Testament was settled into its current form by Athanasius, Bishop of Alexandria in 367 AD. And the content of the New Testament was still argued over for a while after that.[2] With scholars now providing public access to the human processes in the making of the Bible, we should take advantage of that access and dive in to learn what we can.

So very many centuries later, "decision" salvation sounds so unnecessary to me as a privileged and safe person. More important, it seems to undercut the message of God's unconditional love. Naturally, if you think you get an eternal romp in exchange for your allegiance today, it's a great deal as deals go. But is it the basis for love freely given to God, rather than commanded or bargained for? And the downside the doctrine creators would have to accept would be the unfortunately persistent literalist slant and an image of God ready to intervene for or against you. In my admittedly amateur speculation, that was a price the new religion may have decided to pay. Of course, they didn't begin with a proverbial whole cloth. When do we ever, aside from cutting out patterns from swaths of perfect fabric to sew a garment? They performed alterations on existing religious thought, while only certain aspects of the new religion were, indeed, actually new.

And so I had my ups and downs with theology. I was not re-entering a quarrel with a faith like I suffered in my youth, that struggle to fit myself, what I knew, into an impossible set of doctrines. I was on a much more enjoyable quest to find a legitimate fit for a modern person. Demanding only that the basis would not be my own wishful thinking. No twisting of words, but a legitimately scriptural fit. Even if it's never Goldilocks exact.

2. Wade, "Fragile Text," D3.

22: Church and Baseball

Our supper trays on our laps, Bill and I were watching baseball. Over the years, I've developed an avid interest, no doubt aided by playing the game in a co-ed league when we were in our thirties. (I'd played first base, and was nicknamed "Stretch.")

"And this pitcher," Bill said, pointing his garlic bread at the TV. "He . . ."

"Oh, I know!" I said, winding spaghetti around my fork. "He tied the M's in knots last time around. But he wasn't as sharp in his outing against the Angels, so we just might shell him." I shoveled in the tomato sauce I'd made from the "scratch and dent" tomatoes—the last of it from the freezer—and followed up by forking up a wilted leaf of basil and a mushroom.

Bill smiled and muttered to himself, "You have learned well, Grasshopper." And to me, "Yup, I bet we win this one, if our bats are working . . . Your spaghetti sauce is really good, Jean Louise."

"I'm glad I put in the touch of rosemary."

I was getting more active again at church, only interrupted by drop-everything episodes of Mom's declining health. I joined a hospitality team for coffee service, and ushered or greeted from time to time. Church services fell into a pattern of their own, in which the venerable mixed with newer ideas that had drawn me here: covenant, community, "kindom" in place of "kingdom," and care for the Earth. Among the newer things I was seeing were the Iona Community hymns, and references to something called Taizé. I could be grumpy about some of what I thought of as the non-modern. So I told myself that even a progressive church—perhaps especially a progressive church—needs a mix of members, with a mix of feelings about historic ways they may be familiar with and may be dear to them. Something for everyone, including the long-timers (40–50 years of membership). Actually, I was finding that here, those in this eldest group are often among the least attached to old formulae. Surprising, perhaps, yet I can think of four nonagenarians right off the bat who have quietly led into newer theology, in discussion groups, or in prayers that they offer.

My own passing moods sometimes affected how words landed on me. My grumpiest episode may have been the Sunday an outside singer was featured. She sang several numbers and finished with what she called an old favorite, "His Eye is on the Sparrow." I knew the song well. That day it ground my gears even more than the previous times I'd heard it. Not only the pressed-rose sentimentality, which by itself might be tolerable. What rankled that day in the mood I was in was the anti-thought murk, and where it led. Obviously the song was meant to comfort. But what happens when the really dark hours arrive, like the shock our congregation sustained at the fiery car accident death of a young church member. The sentiment that an all-powerful person-God sees and protects the sparrow surely must flip at a time like that to the angst-ridden question: How can God let bad things happen to good people?

Was I just looking for trouble that wasn't there? I don't think so. The flip did indeed happen—in the minister's eulogy for the young woman. He was not one of our pastors but seminary-trained. The church was packed to the fire code breaking point—folding chairs were hastily hauled up from the basement to fill the Narthex, where the overflow of guests could look through glass into the Sanctuary. The anger from the pulpit into the loudspeakers where I sat with the overflow crowd no doubt channeled a current that was present in the assembly. I had no quarrel with his expressing anger, not really. It surely is part of lament, of shock, of sorrow. But if I feel the anger could have been directed differently than at God, am I being small? Certainly I know that many Christians manage a relationship with a person-like God. They talk with the deity and ask or demand to know why, and come to some kind of peace. But in the moment at that memorial service I worried that implicating a God who could have, and didn't, save her, would turn off the many high school visitors.

In *Traveling Mercies: Some Thoughts on Faith*, Anne Lamott crafted with great charm and lightness her conversations and tussles with a person-like God. She reported lovely outcomes for herself, and, like her legions of fans, I delighted in her journey—her climb out of substance abuse, her humor, her relationships with the people in her church.

I'm glad for her, for the peace and wisdom she found, and for the way she raised her son. And I'm glad for her writings that entertain us while enriching and updating the Christian conversation. But I worry that Christians writing of the joys of a personal relationship with a person-like powerful God simply can't help those whose faith crashes hard. We all know folks who were in the same person-God nest but were knocked out when up against a hard loss, particularly an atrocious, evil loss, and went into free-fall. These are sincere people who may be unable to hold their image of God a bit lightly like Lamott does, perhaps because there wasn't any lightness in their Christian education, and now they feel deeply betrayed. These children of God are wounded and I wish for them a friend who locates God more liberally, expansively, and can extend a paddle to them and haul them, dripping, into a new boat.

I looked for the passage that inspired "His Eye is on the Sparrow." Starting with the Revised Standard Version on my bookshelf, "Are not two sparrows sold for a penny? And not one of them will fall to the ground without your Father's will." So, to my dismay, the song doesn't stray off on its own. But then I checked the New Century Version, and saw that a sparrow can't die "without your Father's knowing it." Willing and knowing are two vastly different things. God does not distantly decide our fate. How much better, as in this church that holds me in its embrace, to let God grieve with us.

If I could not be one of the "direct hand" believers, what *did* I believe about God? God to me is not a person writ large, with hands and feet, except metaphorically. One day in a church book club the question came up—who or what is God to you? I cheered when one friend and lay leader said she saw God as "a luminous web." Others that day said, "the ground of our being," or "the universal source." To me, God is ineluctable. A vastness, intimate, wondrous, good, supportive, like the presence I felt that day at the beach.

I have never heard "Sparrow" called for at FCCB, though it is in the hymnal. Similarly, our Sunday prayers don't promise a shield from heartache, pain, or death, or ask us to accept God's mysterious will. Instead our prayers call for spiritual healing, and hope for new eyes with which to see the world. I find that to be nurturing. But I don't want to forget that somewhere along the line, this was a change.

There needs to be room inside Christianity for all backgrounds, so I also need to be on board with supporting a fellow Christian whose image of God is an intentional being. Just because it's not my way doesn't make another's way wrong. I know that making a personal relationship with Jesus or God can be a way of taking one's religion into daily life and finding comfort and focus in it. How the mind works in different people, even in the same person at different times, can be a source of division; the challenge is not to let it obscure the deeper source of humanity that does unite us. I have started to look at division through another lens, and am finding that it often can be embraced as diversity—as a strength in a modern society, however frustrating it may be. It surely beats authoritarian thought control.

What happens when change comes to congregations? William Bridges in *Managing Transitions* writes that to change things in the present, you must first honor the past. After all, what was instituted in the past was largely seen as good at the time. Bridges was addressing corporate changes, and we in Group Health sought hints in his slim book to help us handle big shifts— shifts that aimed to respond to new realities. The same active honoring before a big corporate change would apply in any cultural shift. It only makes sense. The last thing you want to do, he said, is denigrate what came before, what people have a lot invested in, and worked hard to build, what they took pride in. And I remembered other advice I'd absorbed in my unchurched years: When you hear something you disagree with, try to find some level on which you might agree. So I made it a game, when I heard or sang something that I couldn't accept literally, to ask myself in what sense I *did* agree with it. Maybe as poetry, or metaphor. The sermons were helping—often they encouraged us, reminded us, of this possibility.

It occurs to me that going to church has something in common with baseball. You get more out of it with experience. With the knowledge you gather over time. I wouldn't be such a baseball fan if I didn't have Bill, the walking baseball encyclopedia, to ask questions of, to check my understanding of what I'm seeing. Such as why the pitcher might choose to place a pitch high or low at a specific point in the count. The great pitch—whether sinker, slider, curve or fastball—is great because of where it is in an artful sequence that keeps the batter guessing. And the pitcher, like the preacher, is not really separate and alone on the mound—the catcher, like those in the congregation, sends signals. The infield and outfield also work with the pitcher as well as each other.

Loads of rules get familiar over time, like the infield fly rule, how it is applied and why. But baseball is also good to beginners. Baseball wisdom starts with: Keep your eye on the ball. The ball may take a funny bounce. When you field a ball, don't throw the ball before you've caught it, or you'll fluff both the catch and the throw. Good advice in anything.

I've wondered if change needs to be gradual to be lasting. I wouldn't want baseball to change much, and not rapidly. It could make what I know suddenly wrong! Recently, Bill and I were watching a game.

"What is that? I only just blinked and now there's a man on second," I said.

"That's a new rule. They are tied after nine innings, right?"

"Right."

"So the new rule is they start the tenth with a man on second."

"Sounds weird. But I guess a way to shorten the game."

"Yup, but only in regular season games," Bill added, ever concerned to be fully accurate. "Not in the play-offs." Whew. I'm grateful for that.

On the other hand, nature's patterns suggest that a wholesale re-ordering can come by major jerks as well as by increments. A U. S. West Coast example is the fault line we live with—there is a big earthquake in our future. Pressure is building up between plates riding on the Earth's mantle. These pressures under the Pacific Ocean near our shores can partially release in a barely-noticed slip and slide, leaving the Pacific, well, pacific. Or, we can get a major earthquake, with tsunami, cracked buildings, broken roads. Then we might not recognize the rearranged landscape, though after the jolt a new stability will inevitably occur and we will get used to it. For churches, too, we just don't know how and when human tides or human tectonic plates will move, shift, and restabilize. For me church has already shifted and I find delight rather than the need to hold tight. I don't need to worry about sparrows. Now is the time to keep my eye on the ball—Jesus' teachings—see them all the way deep into my mitt. And not let other scripture, creeds, and tenets gather in a wad that fills my mitt before the ball can get there.

One more reason to enjoy each new sunrise—to see what happens next.

23: Your Place is in Your Watershed?

B oth my beach clean-up experience and my visit to Gettysburg National
Military Park had shifted my attention toward place—wherever I am at
the moment. I know that having my own home was always the one posses-
sion I unequivocally wanted, and my home remains a joy for me. And when
we're away to Mt. Hood almost every February, the Great Depression-era
Timberline Lodge speaks to me like some kind of ancestral version of home.
Within this lodge in winter, its vaulting center, massive fireplace, hewn pil-
lars and worn-to-satin floors feel unexpectedly cozy despite its size. Inside it
you don't feel small—you feel an embrace like that of a big brother.

In 2014 in mid-summer came a story about another place. In the Ojai
Valley of southern California, Mennonites hoping to start a new ministry
put on a seventeen-day intensive on permaculture, the agricultural method
that mimics natural ecosystems and is largely self-sustaining without plow-
ing. Mennonites have always been known as Christians who are concerned
about peace and justice and known as practitioners of a land-based ethic.
But this was pushing into new territory, especially in adapting their theological thinking to saving places—you may not be able to save the world, but
you can save places, at least the ones you know and love. An important part
of their workshop was reading the Bible "from a permaculture sensibility."
Ched Myers and Elaine Enns called the need for a new ministry "watershed

discipleship," signifying nothing less than a radical re-*placing* of Christianity, along with a re-placing of ourselves, each in a watershed. Myers says in a blog post, "If we . . . commit to returning repeatedly to our sacred stories . . . we can animate theology and practices of watershed discipleship that promote healing, regeneration and resiliency in our churches and in our world."[1] This tingles with hope. This holistic thinking can shift us to a clear-hearted break with our cultural ways of domination—for isn't domination that oppresses people the same, in essence, as that which oppresses nature? But that break in our thinking, that new thinking, must be carried deeply into our hearts. Theology is a vehicle in that way. I'm especially impressed they are applying the concept of restorative justice to their theology, and working on right relationships with their indigenous neighbors.

I'd felt what it is to care enough for a specific place—my town of Bellingham and its waters—I'd spent a lot of hours, though far fewer than others, working to save it from a major coal port. Could my church ever decide to do a large place-saving action? I'd love to join in for it, but I knew not to expect any specific action with any church that had, after all, other reasons for being. My friend Armand reminded me of that, in one of our conversations, though he is supportive of environmental action himself, and devoted a chunk of his retirement time getting a neighborhood activated to see itself as capable of standing up and being counted. Many of us church members were already active in local work individually and in other groups. But I still wanted an initiative to shine the church's light on. My Carbon Master knowledge was getting out of date without much to show for the WSU investment in me. I am pretty sure in one non-church group I shot myself in the foot with my intensity about climate disruption—coming off as a gadfly, an over-heated killjoy, and overall party-pooper at a mini-reunion of women friends from high school.

1. Myers, "Permeneutics!," lines 30–35.

24: Our Congregation Upended

In 2013 Kent unexpectedly gave notice. He and his partner were going back to their former milieu and family on the East Coast. Our second pastor, Tara, shortly also resigned to decamp for the East Coast. In a few months, Kent was gone. Only three years into his pastorship, his leaving sent a tsunami of shock and tumult through FCCB, and cracked the surface of our unity. Even the newer members, who weren't necessarily plugged into everything, could see all sorts of reactions to broken expectations. I saw the hurt in parishioners who felt he had knocked the pins out from under them. My own feelings soon gave way to admission that I was not really surprised. He had seemed larger than life here in this small town. Not truly a permanent fit.

When we moved to Bellingham, Bill and I bought a lightweight 17½ foot canoe for our flat-water future. We left behind our canoe club, whitewater thrills, and our heavy canoe. The new boat is Kevlar with a thin gel coat, marvelously only about 41 pounds, a tremendous break for my shoulders. This boat has set us up nicely for lakes and quiet saltwater bays. Our friends Bill and Chris also downsized their boating about this time— from their sailing craft. They bought kayaks, as did friends Sally and Ted. Kayaks wouldn't work for our bodies, Bill's and mine, and we were happy to be the big boat among water sprites. I thought I was done with being tossed about and possibly flipped overboard.

The six of us had several fine outings as a group. Maybe we got overconfident. We set out for a day together in Seattle, paddling in Lake Union. We planned to put our boats in on the north side of the lake, just before it funnels into the channel that joins Lake Union to huge Lake Washington. We planned to paddle across to our destination—the houseboat community snugged onto the southeast side of the lake, which makes great sightseeing, all the colors, shapes and designs. We made one mistake: we chose July fifth.

You might well imagine that long tall Seattle, bounded as it is by saltwater on one side and Lake Washington on the other, just might be a boaters' haven. You would be right. Many a Seattleite's craft has overnight accommodations and many that parade on holidays are pretty big, though not mega-yachts—Seattle is not that immodest. So it happened that a number of larger craft, anchored in Lake Union on the big night, were still there the next morning having their coffee, until as if at some signal only they could hear, they all headed for "the cut" to Lake Washington, and perhaps home. Hopefully not still drunk.

As Bill and I finished our set-up, we avoided looking at the ominous chop. The kayaks took the lead. They were bouncing on the wakes, but making progress, when we pushed out into the water, frowning at the commotion of what seemed a hundred boats. We decided to try for a gap among the spiffy craft that dwarfed us, their passengers suddenly in a hurry to feel the wind on their faces. But the enthusiastically powered wakes hit us hard, and sideways, a vulnerability in an open canoe.

"This isn't good," I shouted over the noise. The thought of capsizing here was . . .

"Damn scary," Bill said, finishing my thought. "Turn into the waves! Pry!"

I didn't need to be told what to do. And so his paddle applied a rudder while in the bow I grabbed the opposite gunwale and my paddle together, the blade pointing straight down alongside the boat. With my other hand up on the handle I levered away the water. Did this several times. We spun, just what we were aiming to do. Now each wave hit the point of the bow. The canoe rode the wave tops and troughs, bucking and thumping. Almost fun. Except we were soon buffeted by waves from another direction and we found ourselves very busy, digging to make forward progress to get us through this elephant parade and to steady the boat when we weren't maneuvering. We used all the strokes we were so glad we remembered—sweeping, prying, and drawing for me, J-stroke and hard ruddering for Bill, and booking it as we could. But it was still wild and scary. We felt like pedestrians trying to cross five lanes of I-5 traffic.

"Should we turn back?"

"We may have to. But we could dump doing that, too."

"Wait, I see a break ahead."

"Ramming speed!" he commanded. I laughed as I dug hard. How embedded in our marital shorthand movie lines are. The line was from one of those old Technicolor spectacles involving ancient oar-powered ships, and we had found the script funny, the escalating demands made of the sweating slaves, culminating in "ramming speed." Maybe it was the actor's delivery.

We got to the other side of that sloshing bathtub, panting from the effort. Our friends bobbed in calmer waters, waiting to compare notes and expletives.

Ted slid his kayak next to us. Bill stowed his paddle and, wringing out a large sea sponge over the side, asked "How was it?"

From under his damp black mustache, Ted said, "Ask Sally. She's the one who had the James Bond breakfast—black coffee, yogurt, and green figs."

Bill C. called up Swiftian satire. "Yahoos," he said, disgusted.

And Chris: "We were worried about you. You need some kind of outrigger canoe."

Clearly, we didn't want to have to do this again. Maybe bigger lakes are not for us. Unless. Unless we could have something as a stabilizer, like Chris said. It turned out we could fit our canoe with such a thing. Very effective. As long as we are not foolhardy, we can paddle out with confidence.

I don't recall why I did this, not knowing him well, but when Kent invited one-on-one meetings in his waning days with us, I sought a few minutes with him in his office. We chatted easily, both of us relaxed. And then he revealed something that I think church-goers don't often think about. He said, "A pastor can have friends inside his church, but in his leadership position, not the kind of close friends with which you let your hair down, or air your complaints and frustrations to." So three years with us must have seemed long to him, away from his big home city, while the tine was short to us.

Kent's leaving ushered in a prolonged period of rudderless time during which no big ideas could launch. Of course, Sunday services continued to have much to offer, supported by staff and laity and guest preachers, and continued to grow into a habit with me; if Bill and I went away for a weekend, it seemed a long stretch before the next Sunday rolled around. Threads of reverence for places popped up in the sermons of temporary pastor Alan Claassen, who spoke of the peace of wild things, quoting Wendell Berry's "The Wild Geese." You could have heard a pin drop at Berry's words. Alan's sermon took off from Berry's ending words, how, indeed, what we need is here. And if we become aware we are caught up in patterns that tear down the Earth we have? What do we do then? What do we draw on that is already here?

That's when an idea came to me how we could use this interim time and continue working from where we were. After all, we were Congregationalists; we were all part of leadership. Suddenly, confidence bloomed in me as in the child heroine played by Judy Davis in the 1979 Australian film, "My Brilliant Career." If you missed it, it is about a girl growing up in the outback with outsized creative ambitions.

25: My Brilliant Career

It started with the all-church read in winter, 2014. The book was *Take This Bread: A Radical Conversion* by Sara Miles, and Janet O. would lead discussions. Janet is a retired nurse turned professional coach and group facilitator, a devoted FCCB member and bold in a variety of leadership roles, and everything she does is warmed by an elfin charm. All of which is to say she is guaranteed to have an audience when she leads discussions. FCCB for many years had a beneficial though ho-hum response to food bank needs—a monthly collection for the Bellingham Food Bank a few blocks away. Now came *Take This Bread,* about faith and service, but far from ho-hum. Miles is very gutsy, a self-described thrill-junkie. (Sample statement: You are "never more alive than in a war zone.") Reading Miles made me smile to think of her astounding experience in war followed by her return to church as comically parallel with my more pedestrian path of return. She writes: "I'd learn that it's possible to fall in love with a revolution—then doubt it, fight with it, lose faith in it, and return with a sense of humor and a harder, lasting love. I would have to learn the same thing about church when I was much older, and it would be no easier."[1]

1. Miles, *Take This Bread,* 35.

Miles's concerns soon narrowed down to focus on issues of feeding the hungry. She spoke with compassionate criticism of the usual way of feeding the hungry by sourcing foods from an unfair system—"to make bread out of injustice."[2] I eagerly went to the discussion meetings. At the last of these, I pinch-led for Janet, who was double-booked. Most of the interest, it seemed, was around the most concrete idea—opening up a church—our church—for more radical food distribution. Or opening up the basement for something like that. Something big. Chaz had said it back when we did visioning. And then he left. I wished for something big, too, but perhaps more in the nature of a change of heart about our food system, that would lead us to re-jigger our individual buying practices. Effects could ripple outward from our highly social members.

The deep current of feeling for a ministry in the basement would have to wait until we had a settled pastor, but after the last book discussion, I got an idea for this period of waiting. It involved food and justice, one that would build on what was already in people's minds if they'd read *Take This Bread*. As my idea began to take shape, I gave myself a reality check. What I had in mind would have to be unlike my previous enviro projects that had no obvious connection to the social justice interests of the congregation. Green Team had sat on the margins of the church, after all. Our help with recycling, our boostering of ride-sharing, and cheering for the building energy audit and retrofits were a start. And I'd had a good number attend my talk before worship one Sunday after Earth Day. But the anti-coal port effort was too big, too hard to digest. I had to admit that fears of controversy sometimes could be borne out. Deb, of Bellingham Unitarian Fellowship, told me that taking a stand for Lummi Nation did lose them a few members. But then they gained other members.

FCCB had been through a lot, in being full-throated on the leading edge of marriage equality, and in losing so many pastors. Was there another way for this congregation to move forward in this interim time?

The idea I had for the spring wasn't controversial and it was only a small step. I couldn't find a flaw in it. Though I personally was a bit fragile that spring—in February I had suffered a traumatic fall into a snow fissure while mountain snowshoeing. Not only was I wrenched and strained physically, but rescuers couldn't find me while I clung to the top edges of the mini crevasse by a heel and an elbow, my legs splayed to cramping. I hung on for quite some time and came close to slipping into what might have

2. Miles, *Take This Bread*, 149.

THE RIVER BEYOND THE DAM

been a snow burial. This frightful experience I relived for, oh, about a year. I was still in physical therapy, but I felt I could surely do a small project at church, with a bit of help.

For those who'd read *Take This Bread*, we already had started a broad Christian exploration relating to food. Food had potential for loosening our stuck situation in this time of temporary pastors and waiting. More vitally, my project would "go" without my having to attempt to steer it. I felt it couldn't fail. Hadn't Benjamin and Rosamund Stone Zander said, in *The Art of Possibility*, that all of our fellow travelers are like an orchestra? And that leadership doesn't need a podium, but can come from the musician sitting in any chair.[3] I basked in a vision of a congregation coming together in a small action while we waited for a new permanent pastor. It seemed the time was right. Certainly the spring season was right for interest in food and growing things. All it needed was a good introduction, a few organizers, and continual promotion. I knew how to do the latter well enough, from my old job in community relations and communications.

The idea was—drum roll—"Justice at the Table." At its simplest, merely an exploration of food justice issues, adults and children learning one new thing apiece over the late spring and the summer, on a topic of their choosing. That last part was the brilliant part, so wide open that everyone could follow their own bent while participating together. The service-oriented could learn about immediate services—such as the food bank or the gleaning program. The big-picture folks could learn something new about upstream systemic issues. And we would all gain insights into how our individual favorite issues intersect with labor, trade, racism, women's rights, soil conservation, pollution, health. At the end of summer we'd have a special Sunday service devoted to this food justice learning theme, and a picnic. If enough organizers joined the effort, we could also have a fair with exhibits. Or we could simply take twenty-second turns at the pulpit on the culminating Sunday just to say "My question was. . . I learned that . . ." Participation could be as easy as a few clicks of the mouse on a search engine, or it could be more involved, such as learning to grow vegetables, which I knew Scott D.'s family was already doing, or delving into connections between poverty and the dominant food system, an interest I was sure some others must have.

Justice at the Table could keep the heat on what was already percolating. I was so excited. And instead of having to herd cats, since I knew

3. Zander and Zander, *Art of Possibility*, 76.

we were a busy congregation with many subgroups each doing their own thing, the project would celebrate our very lack of herd behavior, our very lack of a big new initiative to focus us. I wouldn't have to lead, only collaborate and make the weekly email teasers fun. I would show in my Sunday displays an even-handedness, so I would be assuring any conservatives that I wasn't trying to push, say, a moral case for veganism, or boycotts, or letter-writing, or any other idea. No push but to bring us together, engage us all, learn from each other. And watch our garden of compassion grow. The spring and summer calendar looked pretty open. A couple of us from A Just Peace went to the Mission and Justice Board in March, and the board agreed to sponsor.

I met with our temporary pastor, Alan, and salmon activist Wendy. If I had been listening, this was when Alan warned me that he wouldn't have much time left in his contract to provide much support. What I *heard* was an assignment I could start on right away—his preference that I launch initially in the monthly newsletter, the "Full Circle."

Justice at the Table started with some handiwork—the church didn't have the kind of upright free-standing display structure I needed. So I rummaged through our garage, which is an oversized storage locker for all the things we are reluctant to toss out. Well, in the case of an iron cook stove with mint green and cream enamel that had seduced Bill in an antique shop, some of the things aren't easily toss-able. I found the frame of a room divider screen I'd built years before. "Built" implies it was sturdy. It wasn't. A couple of reinforcing screws, however, and it would serve if handled with care. Onto the thin wooden frame I tied fabric panels cut from a cotton tablecloth, and pinned on my first display.

Palm oil was one of two topics—what happens to the rural people and the land when agribusiness is single-minded on export, clearing trees and displacing people. Local versus shipped-in foods was the other topic. I was thinking of lemons, which I've been told are typically flown here, using jet fuel much nastier than truck fuel, though I wasn't going to bring out that part. I set up my display in the social hall for coffee time.

I didn't want to trust to the magnetism of my display, or to luck. So after the kick-off in "The Full Circle" with an invitation to join the Justice at the Table activity, and after preparing my coffee hour display, I baked two trays of verjuice bars. They looked just like lemon bars. I was glad that Mount Baker Vineyards had picked up on an emerging market—our Whatcom County climate doesn't really have the kind of heat and sun to ripen white wine grapes, but under-ripened ones make a great lemon substitute. I cut the treats small, recruiting help when the effort to cut through the hard short-bread bottom was making my bad right shoulder grind and pop uncomfortably. I placed a placard by my little treats on the serving table, describing them as made with sour, unripe wine grapes instead of lemons—an example of how we can, if we want to (or perhaps if we need to in the future) make do nicely with local produce. Of course, the placard also directed people over to my display for some of this information.

As I was sliding several of the bars onto a plate to carry over to my display, Kathi M. stopped by and took one. I was only lightly acquainted with her, but she seemed an active, can-do committee type, who recently had been drafted into the prominent role of church moderator for the year.

"These bars, how do you say it? Ver-juice?" She said "ver" to rhyme with ware. Perhaps she took Spanish in school like I had.

"That's right, or you can say VUR-juice. It comes from the French vert for green."

"They are delicious. They do taste lemony. This theme—food justice and the environment—this is exactly the type of thing that would bring my daughter to church if anything would. She's twenty-five and doesn't go to church, not even when we visit her in Seattle for the weekend."

I returned to my display, thrilled that someone like Kathi had such a favorable reaction. I was sure that it would translate into enthusiastic participation all around. At my homemade standing screen with large-print blurbs pinned onto the panels, a couple came by. They were newer, perhaps regular visitors like I once was. We talked and they sounded already hip to the issues I was highlighting. They were also darling, a well-matched pair. Well, how can I call them darling as though they were young, when they were only about ten years younger than I was? Then Larry M. came by; he knew a speaker on a closely related topic, for my mental file. Larry moved quietly and competently among us, trying to get solar on the church roof, but didn't leave it at that—he had a project at home to connect his solar panels so his electric car could be charged by solar power. But mostly people stood off and talked with friends and met new folks, a coffee cup in one hand and maybe a plate in the other with chunks of cheese, crackers, grapes, and an un-lemon bar. Or they sat at one of the round tables, because, well, it's hard to eat anything while standing with a cup in one hand and a plate in the other.

I didn't know it then, but the limited success of that day would prove not a strong beginning, as I hoped, but already the high-water mark of the project. The tea leaves I should have read were in the droves who stayed away from my display, sitting at tables for general conversation. And why would they not go straight to coffee and conversation? Still, I plowed ahead cheerfully, convinced this was just the start. With repeated exposures, people would flock to the theme. They surely would. The next Sunday I displayed a couple of paragraphs on the two sides of beef, no pun intended—how some say we should run fewer cattle, eat less beef, and others say that some agricultural spots around the world are too hilly, rocky, or dry for vegetable crops (like parts of our Midwest that are natural grasslands), so some raising of animals for meat makes sense even into the future. I had "the two sides of bananas" ready for the Sunday after that.

I soon realized that the displays that were effective at coffee hour were quick sign-ups, bake sales, and the festive annual Board Fair that completely took over coffee time. Not what this lone woman was doing. And this lone woman was not even one of the leaders. Dottie D., a revered elder among us and lifelong peace activist, told me my paper postings on my room divider were too small to read despite an 18-point font or bigger, and required too much reading (even two paragraphs was too much) for coffee time. Hmm. I guess so. One or two people at my urging took my reminder slips about picking a question to study up on. I checked with a person here and there: Had they seen the info about the project in The Full Circle? Blank looks, confessions they hadn't read the church newsletter. And, of course, lots of people skipped the coffee social time altogether, conversing in the Sanctuary or Narthex, or attending to tasks such as tearing the attendance sheets from our red fellowship folders if they were ushers, or leaving church to get on with their day.

Between monthly Full Circles I put blurbs into our weekly e-news asking for organizers, pitching how easy it could be to plan for a picnic or for the finale Sunday service. I contacted the youth coordinator, and the children's programming minister, and laid plans with them. Dear Meril D. volunteered to do a Time with Children on the food theme, and that was good. However, no one showed up to the youth meeting the evening I brought chocolate chip cookies, with chocolate chips that had a story to tell—chocolate harvested without all-too-common coercive child labor. At that moment in time, the youth group was small. In a short few years we'd have a thriving youth group, so this was just the luck of the draw. But it was more evidence that zero momentum was building for Justice at the Table.

Everyone was so busy. A prime example was Meagan D., the woman who sent me an article validating that food was at the intersection of almost any major issue you'd care to name. Meagan couldn't help because she was working on her PhD as well as her full-time job. And her husband, Scott, eminently a greenie by education, now had more of the family duties, as well as leading his family's first garden project, to see how well they could feed themselves from what they could grow. I thought, great! They can be a very interesting part of the sharing we'll eventually have, according to this vivid vision of mine, as a congregation.

But over the weeks of continued displays, newsletter teasers, and meetings with A Just Peace, nothing of my vision was really happening. Some of the real doers of the church were working almost full-time to get us the right new pastor, and the built-in work of the many boards was keeping others busy. I was guiltily unaware of some of their projects, and the projects I did know about were lovely ministries. But that was why I was working so hard to show that Justice at the Table would be an easy, fun thing, not time-consuming. I heard that Diaconate had a picnic idea and that I'd better contact their leader. So I did that. Did everything, in fact, that I or my sponsors thought of.

26: Hitting the Skids

T he weeks went by and I had no one joining in, my dismay increasing steadily. Alan had only a few months left in his pastoral contract. I sent him material to consider for the Sunday finale.

"Thanks, Jean," he answered, "How is the picnic coming along?"

"Oh. We don't have a leader for it yet. Or a committee, actually."

"Isn't it time to get the picnic going?" he said gently. "Is it time to lower your sights, Jean? On the rest of the project." Of course it was time.

Earlier, I had been encouraged to go to the church council despite my misgivings that it really wasn't church council business whether a project like mine succeeded or failed. I prepared a mini-kit on the project for inclusion in the council's pre-meeting packet, and sent it to the moderator I'd spoken with.

Then everything that could go wrong did.

The meeting night came. It was a big group, around a large ring of six-foot tables in the basement under a low ceiling and fluorescent lights. I didn't understand the discussion, with long silences, about Alan's offer to extend his contract, and I grew tense. When my short spot arrived, I began by referring to the Justice at the Table material in their packets. They gave me blank, quizzical looks. Oh, no. With the moderator having been called away out of town, somehow my materials didn't make it into the council meeting packet.

My instinct, from my experience in middle management, was that if these execs aren't prepared for this, and I'm not prepared to find out what they know and don't know about the project in my short allotted time, then I should cancel out.

But while I sat trying to process this surprise situation (surprises aren't fun for me), Alan jumped up and offered to quickly make copies. Dumbly, I nodded acceptance and struggled talking through the next few minutes. Finally, with Alan back and me stumbling, one council member, Larry G., a middle-aged crew-cut stalwart, asked with directness why this was even before the council. Others must have been thinking the same.

Time was up, anyway, and I almost appreciated this direct procedural. But I was so tied in knots by then, I spoke too flatly. "You're right, Larry. We're done here." I immediately knew it sounded testy. It was testy. With that unintended moment, my emotions flooded me, and I left. As if to reinforce my silly belief that I was in a hole I'd never get out of, only one council member spoke with me at the next Sunday coffee, and she looked at me searchingly, as if I were a mental patient needing kid-glove treatment. She softly said Larry's question hadn't been the nicest, to which I quite honestly replied, "Not at all, Larry was right." Other than this one reach-out, there was polite silence.

I might have learned from my canoe, but in that moment I didn't. Our canoe, covered and strapped down atop Bill's car, was unbeknown to us rammed in a parking lot. The culprit had to be someone's truck with ladders on top sticking out. This was the only explanation for the peculiar caved-in damage that didn't touch the car. The canoe was repairable. It took a trip to Canada, new metal gunwales and some straightening and patching, but we are back on the water. "We're all riding around in patched-up boats." This was from someone who knew all about us Americans. Jennifer James spent a number of years as a medical anthropologist with the University of Washington Medical School and in the 1980s her columns in the Seattle paper were touchstones for me. Her wisdom, too, I forgot when I was overwhelmed with self-disgust and needed patching up.

I was down to the picnic. At the Just Peace group I sniveled and begged for help and also went to the Mission and Justice Board. Both groups responded, bless them. And so, giving up my dreams for a special Sunday—the dream that a good chunk of the congregation would participate, everyone learning something new, paying attention to the justice issues in their grocery shopping carts—I was now leading only a small picnic with a small, down-graded theme. I boosted the picnic from the pulpit on a Sunday two weeks out, simplifying the theme down to foods that tell a story. A story could be when you first learned of a connection between and food and a justice issue. Or, maybe you'll bring Aunt Elsie's legendary Indiana church picnic dish, or there's a local farmer you know, or maybe you grew it yourself. Somehow I got a laugh or two, and drew some interest, seeing it in people's eyes, and in the subsequent sign-ups. Alan later told me, smiling, that I surprised him with the humor. Yes, I guess I had been humorless recently, earnest, selling.

The August picnic was deemed a modest success on its own terms, held on the generous sloped lawn of Stacy and Bert a few miles north of Bellingham. We positioned tables and canopies, my friend Mark doing a lot of the lifting. More than thirty people participated in the theme, writing on newsprint banners the interesting things about the foods they had brought. Alan's Sunday sermon before the picnic had been good. But it could have been part of so much more. Or maybe it couldn't have, I admitted through my disappointment.

In the next two weeks, with it all apparently forgotten except by me, not a sign or acknowledgment that there ever had been a Justice at the Table project reached me except from the handful that worked on the picnic. My emotions burbled close to the surface. I could only barely keep them tamped down during Sunday services. How I had built it all up in my mind. No doubt I was all the more vulnerable from my not-yet-healed traumatic near-burial on Mt. Hood. But partly it was just me. Tipping over the fount at last was singing "Draw the Circle Wide." As we stood together and sang the familiar words, I was cut to the quick. No one stands alone? Who picked this hymn for a Sunday after my project collapsed? Oblivious to my rawness, everyone sang the rising, earnest, true-believer words about togetherness while I surely *felt* alone. Ashamed to have such a feeling, I didn't want to meet anyone's eyes. What brought me to this place, where I'm an idealistic child who hasn't sold any lemonade after hours in the sun? After these years in church appreciating deep connection, my stumbling blocks lifting, my spirit responding to song, did I not yet really believe in love? Did I expect others to know, even though I hadn't said it, that I felt this was a huge flop and I was a failure?

But when at home I calmed down, I could acknowledge that for every idea that scored a grand slam, several others flied out. Including Larry's first effort about investing in solar panels for the church building—but he would be up to bat again. I looked out onto our tall, green garden. My eye caught the iridescent glass damselfly I'd bought from a church member's sale for charity. On its metal stalk it floats above a patch of Bill's small-leaved Williamsiana rhododendrons, and glimmers.

A *New Yorker* cartoon by Roz Chast sketched me so well I pinned it up in my study. Picture a graveyard monument, the pedestal topped by a statue of a nebbish, brows knit, mouth showing disappointment, shoulders hunched by habit. Engraved in solemn all caps, the monument hails the deceased, whose life was a battle with everything. Me. I was the person battling every little thing, as when I installed new ceiling fixtures in the hall at home, with two bad shoulders, because the fluorescents of the time couldn't be in the fully enclosed fixtures that came with the house. Then soon it didn't matter, as new generations of energy-wise bulbs arrived that didn't care about fixture enclosure.

Healing meant, for starters, mending things with Larry—Larry of the ill-fated council meeting. In the weeks that followed, Larry did seem to avoid me, or maybe he'd forgotten and gone back to not really knowing my face from Ada. But, suspecting he did recognize me and was less than comfortable with me now, I reached out to him in small ways, like the Passing of the Peace we do in the early part of Sunday service, until over time he and his wife Barbara became friendly and trusting again. Supposedly gruff Larry with his no-nonsense crew cut—what a softie he turns out to be—the glass art he makes is a permanent, ongoing fund-raiser, including donation of his supplies, for Inter-faith Coalition. The iridescent damselfly rising above the rhododendrons in the garden was made by Larry.

I had been perplexed by the story in Genesis of Jacob wrestling with God, getting his hip dislocated and still he wouldn't let go. The story goes that as the dawn approached Jacob believed he would see the face of God and then must die, so he refused to let go until he'd been given a blessing. The blessing was a new name, Israel, meaning "one who strives with God." Maybe this was my time of wrestling with God. I would do so, I thought, on my own, outside the church walls. I didn't seem to have enough love for church up close, or any sense of humor about myself right now. I kicked myself for my lack of grit when I thought of the true grit of a friend.

My friend Zoe had taken "Grow where you're planted" to heart—admirable but hard for her, as she stuck by her lifelong Methodist church, and she spoke out there against their beliefs in the sinfulness of homosexuality. Hard, because she was in a same-sex marriage herself. The gentle congregation I was a part of was by comparison so easy to be with and work with. And it had given me the gift of sweetening my understanding of Christianity. But at least for my activism I needed to step outside. And take a break.

27: Outside

I even wondered, briefly, if I should do as my friend Jamie did. She had told me, as I said, that her religious life is reduced to praise and gratitude, and any effort she makes in areas of justice and the Earth takes place in her secular life. I wasn't going to abandon FCCB, not by a long shot, but I got busier outside. With a friend, Mary, who is something of an expert in the zero waste movement, I put on an eight-session interactive series for The Willows retirement residence. I have always enjoyed working with seniors, and our series, "Willows Go Green," was a lot of fun, from informative videos to discussing how to reduce paper junk mail.

I joined the League of Women Voters, and did a few things with them. I'm full of admiration for them, and I have liked getting acquainted with these very sharp and engaged women and men. But the lengthy meetings, woof. I also volunteered for the community forum newspaper, becoming a minor editor and proofreader for them. After getting the hang of a piece of software, and the rhythms of preparing events articles, I enjoyed this new small job and its connection to the wider community.

There is nothing like a bit of distance for perspective. Church had been stealthily at work on me. Could I credit an increase in patience to the church I continued to attend nearly every Sunday? I did notice I was becoming more relaxed in places like the stores I shopped in. Typically closed to strangers in my hurry, now I noticed when other people gave me a lift by their attitude, and I tried to let those ripples pass through me, unobstructed, and into others. In Fred Meyer one day (a grocery, drug and household chain), I got into the fast lane with my few items and it slowed to a stop while a bent woman picked through her handbag, her coupons, and her coins to pay her bill. To lift the pressure of our staring, my gaze turned onto the magazine rack, and I commented to the person behind me about a cover photo of the actor Ann-Margaret. He responded, was friendly. The bent woman perked up and said, "She was a *fox*." All were included, all chuckled, and it was probably the highlight of my day.

During this time, 2014, came the awful August events in Ferguson, Missouri. I know Ferguson is some time ago and other horrific racial murders have grabbed us since. But one aspect of these social shocks clung like a burr under my saddle, not allowing its skin-scratch to heal. Bear with me, now—this will not be a rehash, or a feel-bad sermonette. What do you do with an event like the apparently unprovoked killing of a young Black man by a white officer, *followed by strong support given to the officer*?

On an evening soon after the Ferguson killing, amid news of massive street protests, Bill and I saw TV coverage of a counter-demonstration in support of the officer who killed Michael Brown. We saw a woman in mirrored aviator sunglasses speak from a platform, presumably to a like-minded crowd. When this white woman, probably in her thirties, called for support for the officer, Darren Wilson, what struck me was what she locked together. She joined her appeal for support to a categorical statement that his action was "justified." This is what got under my skin. Not only that she provided zero evidence justifying his action. It was the linkage itself, as if the officer can't receive support any other way, and the support can't wait even for manufactured evidence. *Must* she declare him justified regardless of the facts, and say he did nothing wrong? If she felt compelled to offer a culturally shared foundation for supporting him, then we all have work to do. We've heard it before, and outside of race troubles: "If they got arrested, they must have done something wrong." I used to tsk-tsk at the smug ignorance of this attitude, an attitude that immediately dismisses the accused from the fold. That attitude, to the extent it may be widely shared, cuts two ways. Look how we clamor to remain in the "good" group. We don't want to get cast away like we are so ready to do to others.

Tagging the ignorance in such attitudes doesn't do it for me anymore. And yes, it is important to label racist behavior as racist, and not excuse people for racist behavior. But it also no longer works for me to label people and stop there, as if by labeling I've done my job. I want to see hearts soften and change. I want to put on my sociologist hat, and ask, Is this a pattern—even outside of racial violence?

How and when does supporting someone mean you have to declare he or she is in the right? Is justified? What was really going on for Ms. Mirrored Sunglasses to make that linkage simply had to be an upwelling of unmanageably strong emotions that threatened to engulf the crowd in shame. Or in fear, fear of great damage to their world, their town and its settled order, even if the social order is an ugly caste system. You may be thinking, Yeah, I get it, White Fragility, end of conversation.

But I'm suggesting that a defensive impulse to justify one of our own runs deep, even aside from American racism. You may know that justification is built into our criminal law as a proper defense—Wikipedia, under the category Justification and Excuse has this example: breaking into someone's home [an illegal act] during a fire in order to rescue a child inside is justified.

Now take this idea out of the courtroom. Is it strange to think that admitting a wrong action by someone in your group, even a horribly wrong action, could feel like the sky is falling? In my experience, and probably in yours, it really isn't so strange. It's not just there in Ferguson. It's in both the huge geo-political arena and at the small family level. A justification defense is invoked in military actions, of course. Sometimes the bids for justification in the court of public opinion hold up, such as reasons to jump into WWII, and sometimes the reasons don't hold up so well, like "weapons of mass destruction" supposedly found in Iraq. But on the ground, always, these military actions unsettle people even if they don't experience the destruction first hand. You may recall the U.S. made an ill-conceived decision to move the U.S. Embassy in Israel. The Israeli celebrations for the grand opening in 2018 went bad, and ended with dozens of Gazans killed. The next day an Israeli citizen, clearly anguished, was quoted as saying, "When we hear of the dead, it pains us. I hope at least that each bullet was justified."[1] What else could this citizen do but hope? At least he was able to hold in his mind the mixture of pain, doubt, and hope, unlike the empathy-free arrogance we are familiar with in America.

Now comes the part where I am going to suggest a religious background for our justification meme, and how it affects us today, even atheists,

1. Kershner and Halbfinger, "Israelis Reflect," A1.

after we thought the religious part was well and truly laid to rest in favor of the rational and the secular.

The word "justify" in my Merriam Webster leads with: "To prove or show to be just, right, or reasonable. Absolve." But that's not all. In the same way that the public murder in Ferguson brought out very old race reactions, it may have brought out old religious thinking as well; an older definition seems to have nosed its way back in the emotional aftermath. Webster lists it as archaic: "To judge, regard, or treat as righteous and *worthy of salvation*" (italics mine) .

But how archaic is it if it's still much-referenced in the New Testament of the Bible?

I think about how often I don't merely prefer to be seen as having acted reasonably, but feel I *need* to be in the right. Seems like that old definition is still today giving an extra zing to our modern sense of the word justify. We can be despised, shunned, and drummed out of our committee, our neighborhood group, even a bigger social grouping, treated like the unwashed, the unsaved. For minor infractions of formal or informal rules, this social treatment may only be the cold shoulder. It may not be permanent, but it can cause pain even so. I have felt the averted eyes after having spoken in anger, or even with abruptness at an innocent someone. (Or even a deserving someone. Here I catch myself using this justification linkage.) I felt the pain of being in the wrong after my reaction to Larry G. at the church council meeting. Feeling that if I'm in the wrong, it's not only my behavior but my very self that feels besmirched.

On the night previous to the newscast about Ferguson, the movie "The Horse Whisperer" ran on TV, and a scene struck me for the way it illustrated the meme. The storyline itself is certainly not a common instance—a teen who's been maimed in a horrific accident that cost her friend's life is having trouble healing. But the story's solution is a commonly prescribed one. She can't heal until a trusted elder—Robert Redford, no less!—tells her, "Grace, you did nothing wrong."

Now, of course that was a good thing to say to young Grace. The accident involved no tangled backstory of previous actions and multiple causes. But I still have to ask a question, in light of the fear we feel if we have caused, or may have caused, a bad outcome. What if she *had* done wrong? Would we cast her out? In answering, we quickly protest No, we wouldn't! She's a young, darling, sorrowing child we want to fold into our arms.

But take that fearful, grieving emotion and scale it up to social groups and it feels like the sky will fall. We fear the sky will fall if we don't re-stabilize our world quickly and with whatever force or harshness it takes in order to feel that we, or our kind, did nothing wrong.

Do we ever ask ourselves whether we can do better than that sky-is-falling reaction? We can do better. We can acknowledge that we may all have a part in the cultural contradictions that lie behind the wrongful action of one of us. It could be us next time. And we can begin to do things differently, with love, or at least respect for each person's humanity.

An incident in my family some years back was minor but emotionally charged, and may shed a tiny ray on mechanisms at work in bigger social convulsions. An elder having problems with frustration (all right, it was my mother) had ordered her ten-year-old grandson to eat everything on his breakfast plate, which he had politely declined to do, saying the eggs had gone cold. After a short escalation, we watched in disbelief as she stepped over to him and seized him by the ear as though to force feed him. Others then leapt up to his defense. Defending him was, of course, a good response.

But to bark at our mother with faces twisted in anger and horror was a less-than-good response, and that also happened. The boy, my nephew, was soon surrounded by supporters and Mom slumped back, isolated, broken. Then one daughter (all right, it was me) darted to her in support. Though fearful that her nephew would think she was siding with the behavior of her mother, she was more fearful of her mother's collapse, all alone, everyone punishing, discarding her. The family slowly was restored—all members supported—without having to re-make Mom's actions into justifiable actions. If we had tried to make her actions justifiable it wouldn't have been taken as honest, let alone necessary. But then again it was a family matter, where there were strong ties, not a public fight among strangers as in the Ferguson demonstrations. Still, I like to think that restorative justice within a family is a small version of what public justice could be.

Christians could help make it so, rather than throwing others away. A Bellingham writer, James Wells, has said there is no Other. There is no Away. That would make a good starting point.

Patterns. During a sermon long afterwards, recognition sparked, unrelated to what I was hearing in the moment. I saw the kaleidoscope settle into a starburst stained glass pattern. In my past rejection of Christianity, I found fault. Yes, so stipulated. The only choices I'd seen were to justify the faults (make myself wrong and the particular Christian teaching right), or to reject the whole. Is this what's been going on in our cultural wars? Rejection of church on the coasts, while the heartland doubles down on the fearful judgment of the ghost of Christianity past?

28: Back in the Boat

A friend who'd attended Bellingham Unitarian Fellowship for a while
told me she quit when she found they were people like all other
people—she had the same frustrations with them as with other groups. I
didn't want to leave FCCB simply because of an insight like that, and I felt
it was only true to a point—over the years I've had a few bad neighbors,
bosses, and work-mates, and nothing like that among my church fellows.
My feelings about First Congregational and its members were not neutral. I felt, and feel, only affection for them. The Jesus stories provided
me a secure anchor like the blanket did that day in catching my feet. An
anchor not weighing me down; more like a rudder steadying me, giving
me confidence. There were surprising joys, too. I knew this place. I knew
the name of the seeing-eye dog that accompanied the man who split his
Sundays between the Presbyterian church and FCCB. From where I sat
on Sunday I could see Nora the dog working to maintain her patience on
her bed on the floor. I watched how one Sunday she inched and stretched
until she could lay her head down on the sneaker of a parishioner in the
row behind. Who smiled and held her foot still. I caught her eye and
enjoyed the secret moment with her.

Some encouraging currents flowed under the surface of our kum-
by-yah Sundays. At long last, we called a new permanent lead pastor to

replace Kent. Sharon Benton, already introduced back in Chapter 10 because I couldn't wait. She began with us January, 2015. I was a weary church-goer at this time, but I liked her right away. She was energetic and still youngish, like Kent, but unlike him had already spent many years in the Western U.S. It felt as if she and her partner could find a comfortable home here for the long term.

Another fresh current gave us a bounce. An interracial couple in their late thirties, Tiffany, a Black woman, and Mark, a white man, put on a discussion series. Mark and Tiffany M. had been quiet regulars for a while, and while I'd spoken with them, I wondered how it felt to be Tiffany sitting with a sea of mostly white people, few people of color and only one other Black person in attendance at that time. The series Tiffany and Mark brought us did not address race relations, but did make a powerful discussion about slavery, taking off from the story in Exodus. The first meeting drew a big circle of people to the chapel room where on other days a labyrinth was laid out, painted on canvas. No tables, just a circle of chairs.

I went out of curiosity, expecting just another discussion. In Tiffany's hands, however, the story of the Exodus from Egypt crackled like a campfire. She led right off with: This is a story of slaves. The heart of the story is how a great many of the Hebrew slaves feared making things worse for themselves if they left Egypt and struck out, with nothing, for the unknown. Well knowing the story, I said to myself that their fears were reasonable—they were chased and encountered bad water and a shortage of food.

I don't recall whether Tiffany spent much time in the exact territory that Jennifer Yokum had preached on. What I remember is the discussion that blossomed when Tiffany invited us to consider in what ways we might, here and now, feel enslaved despite our evident well-being? Now, I don't think a white person would have dared use the word metaphorically, when the literal meaning of slavery still weighs heavily in our national history, and brooks no comparison. But she could and did. I felt it was incredibly generous of her. Her second question was the other side of the coin: In what ways do we fear leaving bondage?

Where was Tiffany going to lead us? But in inviting us to open up, she succeeded beyond what I thought was possible. Passion flowed forth, expressed variously in chagrin, regret, and recognition of prior social constraints. And longings. Really strong longings. And I was grateful for the heart-talk that happened that day and the following Sunday. Clearly, all of us were awash in gratitude.

A church member named Fred W. sat quietly through the first part of the series. He was tall and straight-backed, yet not giving off the impression of physical strength, nor, to my knowledge, had he ever volunteered in church. He always seemed to have a thousand-yard stare over the tops of the heads of the crowd. I wondered if this stemmed from his years shepherding real estate shoppers, or maybe . . . was it wistfulness?

This same Fred upended my impressions of him in the Exodus discussion. He confessed he was hungry to make amends, as he put it, for not having done more in his youth for social justice. And then some weeks later, to my surprise our pastor was calling him up to the front to receive the congregation's blessing and farewells. He was on his way to Guatemala for three months, having joined the Peace Corps for the *second* time in his life.

I turned to seek the eye of his wife Peg, sitting directly behind me, as Fred got up and came forward, and she smiled back at me, a proud, shining smile that acknowledged that this was surprising to many of us and that she would miss him but it was only for three months and she would be fine and Fred would be fine. All that with her eyes. On leaving the building that day, I looked more closely at the polished stone bench in the little entry garden and saw inscriptions that honored church members' Peace Corps participation, including Fred's.

Rod M. is another older man who at first seemed to be taking it easy in retirement, until I learned that for the past thirteen years he'd led The Jesus Seminar every other Thursday afternoon, continuing the scholarship and teaching he'd started in his career as a pastor. The sessions I sampled comprised an earnest reconsideration of Jesus, with attendees from both inside and outside our church, focusing first on what could be determined about the historical Jesus, and then on to the brave and incisive Don Cupitt and his *Creative Faith: Religion as a Way of Worldmaking*. The sessions also introduced me to Diana Butler Bass, who, in a video, had refreshing things to say about where the Reformation messed up, about how words matter, and about a new story for those who have given up on the story of a transcendent God above. She said the historically smaller thread in theology, that of an immanent (with us) God is on the rise again. That not only matches my religious feeling, but I see it in popular usage among those who don't identify with an institutional religion. Thank you, Rod, for holding these sessions.

To my very incomplete list of local church members I admire, add a woman I'll call Gina. With a full-time job and a daughter in high school,

Gina has worked for years on sensible gun regulation. Her cheerful buoyancy gives no hint of the betrayal she suffered from a favorite uncle in Montana. He disowned her for voting for Hillary Clinton, just and only that. And this uncle and aunt have treated her far worse than a stranger ever since. A stranger could come to their door and perhaps be invited in, while Gina has been told never to darken their door again, a stance that hasn't weakened years on. What they have lost by casting her out! Gina has an exquisite comic side. Remember when "snowflake" was a new insult? She was at the pulpit for I forget what purpose. She turned her time into a hilarious monologue taking off from the sly pretense that she thought snowflake was a compliment.

Barbara, Larry's wife, runs Fresh Start, collecting new or nice household goods to give to newly housed families. And then there is the group of lay members in what is called the Stephen Ministry. These angels are trained and available for support to those having a hard time of one kind or another. A wonderful ministry not just anyone can provide.

Some contributions are more tangible. With choir seating on terrace-type levels that were too shallow to be safe, Jerry C. and Roger S., assisted by Darlene M. and David F., worked their finish carpentry magic, rebuilding and matching the light maple flooring.

Several members have adopted children and are raising them with tender care. Other adults do community work that must be done, serving on nonprofits and commissions—mitigating domestic violence, helping with climate campaigns, human rights and peace work. One family man, Scott D., drops everything when Search and Rescue calls him, a diver, to recover the body of a drowning victim. I am sobered to think of that emotional labor, but it is crucial to the bereaved families.

Young people in this church are also very impressive. And get listened to. I have to mention our debt to Erin J. who carved out a substantial time commitment while still in high school, or just graduated, to serve on a search and call committee. Likewise Kenzie K. who served on the next committee about three years after. These two committees called our present pastors.

The author of one of my favorite modern hymns, Thew Elliot, is a white man associated with a Black church, and when he wrote "Spirit, I Have Heard You Calling," his church was taking on the challenge of accepting LGBT individuals, some of whom had been secretly in their midst from day one, afraid to be known. I was struck by his saying that those who want change and growth might sit silent—for a long time—before joining behind a change leader. The idea that latency is widespread, likely about many issues in many places, actually encourages me. I could, and once did, feel disappointment in what I saw as people's lack of courage to speak up. But I was looking at a snapshot of time. I am so much happier seeing hints of a quiet build-up of desire for change in folks' apparent inaction, because over time I have seen many wonderful changes blossom eventually. Patience. Work. Celebrate. Repeat. Still, here I was, after riding the flow of fresh waters within this church, again wondering what my own place, what my own calling, was here. Maybe it was just going to be revealed in hindsight. New people were coming in, and I was coming to be seen, on a good day, as one of the old stalwarts. Krista and Amaléa were gone to other river channels, and Rob was around less; Kathi and Bob M. and Tiffany and Mark had moved to Seattle.

By 2016 my shoulder problems made precarious the simple act of raising a coffee mug. I had my first shoulder replacement surgery that spring. For my recovery, a lengthy period of disability that Bill nursed me through with great kindness, church friend Helen sewed me a couple of small cushions, one simple and flat, the other a cleverly modified roll. These were beyond helpful for the pain when no position allowed rest for long. She also sent a quart of delicious homemade soup. I tried to pay it forward, later bringing soup to a church member who'd suffered the trials of Job, and helping out others as I could. Helen in particular became a lodestar for me. And she brought into the church another woman who became a good friend. I loved Helen McLeod, and when she died suddenly, her absence hit me hard. I hold her example and her memory close.

29: Easter Reclaimed

In the Lenten weeks leading up to Easter 2016, I was thrilled to be able at last to reclaim the joy in the Easter story that every Christian should feel. Among the blessings brought by Pastor Sharon was her telling of the story that lies beneath the story—telling it simply and understandably, and based on scholarship, always important to me. As I settled into my pew each Sunday in Lent, I felt like I was taking this last major part of Christianity out of the shut-away theological cupboard that used to be stuffed full of my questions and objections. Now my cupboard was empty—nothing has to be shut away anymore. Over the course of several Sundays, coordinated with the all-church read, *The Last Week*, by Marcus Borg and John Crossan, she opened up the Christian story. In the years after Jesus' horrific death, his followers sought to find meaning, including a why.

Apparently they lived with the question for a while. First to write a gospel was Mark, some sixty years after Jesus' death, then about ten years passed before the other gospels came to be, each written on a scroll—a reminder that in the absence of books as we know them today, the everyday person didn't have direct access, at least to the written version. Then centuries went by and an ancient borrowed scapegoat story became orthodoxy. It became the story of atonement for sins through Jesus' sacrifice. I don't recall that Sharon spoke as bluntly as Borg and Crossan did in their book.

Sharon's interest was in what happened after that. Borg and Crossan say, after they outline the logic of the substitutionary sacrifice idea, "Hence it is important to realize that this is not the only Christian understanding of Jesus's death. Indeed, it took more than a thousand years for it to become dominant."[1] This orthodoxy once may have supplied the meaning that church members (and leaders) craved. At any rate, it became the leading explanation for God's allowing Jesus' crucifixion. It's obvious that the God concept people were working with was a person-like, omnipotent and interventionist God who could have saved Jesus.

But today, an age, thankfully, of greater economic and social mobility and of sheer possibility, more of us are asking for meaning to be built on not just what Jesus may have died for, but what he lived for. Sharon said that Jesus lived for, and taught, God's Shalom on Earth. If that becomes our focus, rather than an other-world choice of heaven or hell, where might that take us? That day, like a Mr. Rogers for grown-ups (and that's not to be sneezed at; we all deserve a Mr. Rogers), she spoke to each and all of us with simple words. Words to stay with us, to stick, and not just be a pleasant send-off into a nice spring day. Sharon asked us to consider the rebirth that is available to all of us, every spring, even every day.

On Palm Sunday Sharon worked the contrast of the happy palm-frond-waving crowd at Jesus' entrance into Jerusalem and the awful passion that was to come just a few days later. She said, "Shalom speaks of completeness, wholeness." Before the sermon, the lay person reading the text for the day read the poem, "Palm or Passion, Wave or Particle" by Michael Coffey, about the physics conundrum of the particle that can be a wave and the wave a particle.

> If you let paradox be and mystery win
> it is both at the same time all at once. . .
> looking there and then means
> you only see the particle of a fabricated greatness
> but look another way and see the wave of humility . . .[2]

I had declined an invitation to lead one of the discussions about *The Last Week*, hungering as I did for action rather than discussion, for going into depth with the lessons of the previous book rather than moving on to the next. But, along with Sharon's words, this book that I now quickly

1. Borg and Crossan, *Last Week*, 138.
2. Coffey, *Mystery Without Rhyme*, 143.

scanned warmed me. With a sigh of relief, I'm now fully confident I can identify as a Christian without representing old orthodoxy to the non-Christian world. Now I know what is meant by one of the UCC taglines: Our faith is old, our thinking is not. My study of sociology and my Christian upbringing just shook hands—no, hugged each other.

But what's in the Bible—before orthodoxy got barnacled onto the good word? Borg and Crossan, in *The Last Week*, say "We have translated 'ransom' in the book of Mark into sacrificial terms, but it almost certainly does not have this meaning in Mark. . . the Greek word translated as 'ransom' (lutron) is used in the Bible not in the context of payment for sin, but to refer to payment made to liberate captives (often from captivity in war) or slaves (often from debt slavery). A lutron is a means of liberation from bondage."[3] This speaks volumes to me, who tangled with myself as a young person, trying to find more sin to fight in myself, to root out of myself. Trying so hard to be good, I was in a kind of bondage, a captive of harmful elements in our culture, and even of a religious worldview that refused to *accept* the world, as pernicious as that negation became. Never mind accepting women's autonomous lives.

Ironically, now that I found I could have it my way—that I don't need to subscribe to the substitutionary sacrifice tenet—has made me loosen up about other Christians' ways of being Christian. Sacrifice, salvation, the old wooden cross—these have gifts, too, and certainly are a part of the Christian yin and yang, if I can borrow a concept (don't tell my friend Alys). The cross is about sin, but let it be about the systemic sin of a power politics that goes to any lengths to keep a regime propped up.

Why have I never seen that before? This is the social justice reason for church to exist—the challenge alongside the nurturance. And if I couldn't see this before, as a student of culture, it only shows how taken for granted are our American individualistic culture and its American Christian individual salvation.

But it's even better than that. Martha Tatarnic, rector of St. George's Anglican Church in St. Catharines, Ontario, has noticed her parishioners are more comfortable with saying Jesus died for their sins than she is. Her parishioners know something about the power of self-sacrificial love. Another ah-ha for me—Every time we forgive a debt, haven't we sacrificed something financially? Every time parents make a career sacrifice for their child, they know something about this kind of love. Here is where my

3. Borg and Crossan, *Last Week*, 154.

heart joins my mind, and brings me peace. I've always thought of myself as independent, as doing my share, as not having needed anyone's sacrifice for me. But it's not remotely true. And now, free of the doctrine of substitutionary sacrifice, I *can* accept that Jesus set the example of sacrifice—Jesus rode that burro into Jerusalem knowing he went into the teeth of trouble—and did what he did out of love.

This is a quiet return to revolution in Christianity. Since I was coming at my questions as an amateur, I appreciated finding "How I teach theology to undergrads" by Aristotle Papanikolaou of Fordham University. He says: "I try to lead students away from overbearing überstructures designed to force people to think a certain way or think they are never doing enough. Instead, I lead them toward an understanding of being religious that has to do with formation of the person to be in a certain way—a being that is in communion with the divine. Being religious is less about agreeing to certain propositions or following certain rules, and more about transforming one's mode of being in the world. Being religious is very much like being an artist . . . My students are searching for purity. I teach them that they will not find it and that they need to learn to live with ambiguity—even in a liberal democracy, in which lies their greatest hopes. Compare a dance academy with all its flaws that nevertheless turns out dancers. Quality they could not achieve on their own, outside of the institution."[4] The religious arts, seen like dancing! That is so enlightening, and so encouraging.

I again recall Sara Miles in *Take This Bread* saying you can fall in love with a revolution, then lose faith in it, yet ultimately return to it. Christianity was a revolution in its early years. I had fought with what it had become over time, at least what I saw behind dams of stagnancy. I had given up on it, then found my way to another chance to restore my faith and belonging.

So here I am, remaining afloat on this river with my fellow travelers, letting the outgrown fall away like the trees toppled from the banks, sweepers that are only hazardous if you don't paddle around them. I will take time to surf the standing waves and to rest in the eddies.

A June morning, 2018. I wake up at 4:30 a.m., the generous summer light already haloing the edges of the light-blocking roman shade at our heads. (If I could flip the house to bring that east light into the kitchen, I would in a heartbeat.) I can't stop a chuckle from erupting, and then another. Bill is awake, too. I nestle my head back into my feather pillow and wonder why I am laughing. I review the day just past, searching. I'd been

---

4. Papanikolaou, "How I Teach," para 9.

to Paper Dreams, the card and gift section of Village Books, for another package of blank greeting cards. I knew right where to find them, past long aisles of bright single cards for birthdays, weddings, and get-wells, to the back corner of the store where the boxed cards hide, and I picked up sixteen nice modern florals for $10.95. Now in the dawn light I recognize myself. That's it! I've become one of those settled, silver-haired church ladies, a cookie spatula in one hand and a pen in the other for writing condolences or encouragement.

"Well," Bill says with a slow shake of his head at the unaccustomed hour, "I think I'm up, too."

After a breakfast of Scottish oats, blueberries, walnuts and tea, we take my little electric car from our pizza-red house to the Stimpson Reserve, a pristine woodland area just out of town. We walk the Geneva Pond loop, hiking up and down the ridge-and-valley terrain, and arrive at the pond, where we always look for ducks whatever the season. We've seen some honeys. Wood ducks with breathtakingly colorful markings that their name doesn't do justice to. Scaups, buffleheads, mallards, and Canada geese. In the verdant quiet this morning, our footfalls make no sound on the duff-coated trail. Over our heads the sun knits together greening branches of neighboring trees; it will soon take more than a light rain to wet the forest floor. Bill and I each fall into reverie. Mine is: Did I conquer, see and do, that diarist's ambition at fifteen? Another reason for wry amusement. We stand a minute in the early light gazing out at the pond, its surface made interesting by fallen logs. Bill notes the half smile crooking my face as I think of that hungry teenage aspiration, and he waits to see if I will say something. I just beam at him, noticing which of his collection of baseball caps he is wearing—Tacoma Giants, the 1960s minor league team—and I say nothing. Certainly the heights will stay unconquered by me. I guess I did all right even so, and I'm grateful especially for my marriage to Bill, my intimate, my beloved tether. Who, by the way, makes really good coffee, and on this sleepy early morning, strong milky coffee is what I hanker for as we traverse the back side of the loop toward home. Following him in a narrow section of the trail, I spot a critter he'd missed.

"Oh, look, a good fella," I say, stopping in front of a pale olive-green banana slug. I've seen a few dark brown slugs this morning, and am happy to see this native.

"Well, move him off the trail," Bill says, happy at the encounter.

Nodding, I say, "He seems to be headed over here." I employ a fir cone and a winter-dried leaf to scoop him up, almost dropping him as he shrinks, evading touch, and I set him down on the moss bed edging the trail, out of the way of any runner who might dash by.

"Just don't lick your fingers," Bill says with the merriment of the inside joke.

"Nope, there's no toothache to treat today," I say, laughing to recall how I'd taken a dare from a docent in British Columbia's Capilano Suspension Bridge park. The docent called for someone to lick the banana slug we'd come across, to experience how native peoples once had used the anesthetizing properties. What was I to do when I saw my opportunity to pull even with my sister Julie? She was with us that day on a visit from Ohio. Julie had out-braved me years earlier in Australia by answering the call for a volunteer to help shear a sheep. I guess we girls keep score. My tongue went numb and she and Bill cackled. Both refused my offer of a kiss. The numbness lasted three hours. I was assured the slug would be fine.

Now under the green canopy Bill and I continue on, our pace steady, me wishing for another of Julie's visits. And I smile to think that yes, indeed, my teenaged predictions were rather accurate that this part of my life would be modest and settled. But my young self was wrong about what the settled time would be like. Not a giving in, nor a giving up. Not deferring to men, in the family or at church, but standing side by side. Not a negative time at all, even though physical strength begins to wane, but rather a pleasure in being just who and where I am, pleasure in being plugged into life and community, not holding myself apart or keeping to just a few friends and family.

A big part of my pleasure in paddling with this community has come from our second pastor, Davi Weasley. I was there at the formal Saturday ceremony installing them. I remember seeing that Davi's stole slipped, hanging long on one side and remaining uncorrected throughout the ceremony. At the time, this reminded me of the awkwardness of a fledgling bird. Now I can revisit this scene with a new view: simply my first introduction to Davi's almost preternatural ability to stay in the moment, fully with the person in front of them, with no room for self-consciousness.

I think back to when FCCB went through the retooling that dedicated the second pastor's job description to youth, young adults, and mission. There were various trepidations about making a change (what will we lose?). My own trepidation came from concern about Davi's roots in the Baptist denomination, which I took to be uniformly a good deal more conservative than Congregationalists are. And what about "mission" in view of environmental collapse? Then Davi invited me for coffee shortly after they joined us. In the tiny Lettered Streets Cafe I spoke of my belief that unless we had some focus on the Earth, we can't hope to make progress by only helping a trickle of individual humans, as the trickle will become a human flood set to overwhelm us. And, in the interests of honesty in getting acquainted, I admitted the concern I'd had. Davi just drank it all up, listening closely, clearly valuing me. And I was wrong about their Baptist background being so conservative. This was proven to me over Davi's many subsequent sermons. And recently they commented to me that though there are plenty of conservative Baptists, "the ones who helped train and ordain me are mostly as progressive or more progressive than most of the UCC folx I hang out with."

In hiring Davi—scholar, adroit flock tender, and activist in Chicago— we got exactly what we aimed for, and more. And so attuned to younger generations and newer technology, they make a great minister to team up with Sharon. I love them both without reservation. In that kind of relationship, I can sit in complete comfort during Davi's words at Communion, the ones straight out of Matthew (blood shed for us) recited in complete serenity. My thinking about this text hasn't altered but my experience of this church is larger than any one text. I guess I'm over being "stung as a child."

Actually, my friend Kathleen Norris suggests that how blood now abounds in our mass entertainment may be part of my reaction against it in religion. I call this writer my friend on the strength of her history—like me she is a church leaver and church returner. Norris herself finds the hymn "There is a Fountain Filled with Blood" over the top. But she seems to urge patience with historical religious traditions about blood, by pointing out that because Jesus was human, "Blood includes us in the Incarnation—not so crazy, after all, but an ancient thing, and wise. The rhythm of life that we carry in our veins is not only for us, but for others, as Christ's Incarnation was for the sake of all."[5] I'm okay with that. Very okay.

That teenaged girl that I was in 1965 was also not quite right about what a Christian mind could be, and how it could draw from the gift of a deep sweet-water river downstream from national politics. The tumbling waters constantly cleansing our cultural patriarchy and domination ways. Sampling depths of joy, of love, even sometimes honest-to-God peace. And on a lazy Sunday, I may be nudged to go to church . . . by none other than Bill.

5. Norris, *Amazing Grace*, 115.

30: Black Womanists Matter

A worry crops up. All right, with me there is always a worry. I must be kin to the title character in "Joe and the Volcano." I can celebrate the moonlit celluloid moment of Tom Hanks on his makeshift raft bopping to the Del Vikings' "Come Go With Me," and then in the next beat, nod knowingly as worry overtakes him. "It's always going to be something, with you, isn't it, Joe?" Meg Ryan says. Maybe so.

Here's my worry: This reconstruction, this reinterpretation, this refreshed Christianity that I've embraced in a marvelous church (and there must be any number of other marvelous churches) might stand in the way of deepening some new friendships. My old Panama best friend friend I couldn't find, so the issue never came up. But I think of new acquaintances, like Darla, a devout woman of color whom I like a lot. I only met her because my church hosted meetings of a local Black Lives Matter group. It was the fact I was churched, and not simply a member of the public attending the meeting, that interested her in me. I don't want to screw up a new friendship. I worry that it's possible that if she and I talk long enough, Darla might not see me as a proper Christian. Well, I'll just have to feel my way along.

What about the bigger question of Black and white sisterhood? Is it possible that a deeper, more trusting sisterhood between Black and white women can be fostered via church, via progressive theology? I am prompted to ask because of what happened with the Women's Marches.

With the 2016 election, I felt more under threat as a woman than I ever had. I was stunned. Throughout the campaign and continuing after election night, the President-elect and his coterie shock-jocked day by day, even hour by hour, with sneering invective. So much for the campaign being over, so much for returning to some civility. And we'd seen enough already to know this wasn't just so-called locker room talk. I was in good company in my alarm and outrage. As everyone knows, the Women's March on Washington fairly exploded into the streets. I joined Bellingham's march, one of an estimated 408 marches across the U.S., and the biggest march by far that Bellingham had ever seen. Bill bought a yellow and orange safety vest for his role as a volunteer traffic guy. I wore the magenta hat I quickly knitted, cat ears sticking up at full attention. I thought, Yes! We are unified and energized. We are rising up! And we were, and I was thrilled in my every fiber at the sheer happy surprise of it all—the placards in endless homemade variety recognizing the inseparability of women's rights with climate disruption and race issues. Men joining us wholeheartedly, Darla, neighbors, the many church friends happy to see one another making history together. A gentle fierce determination radiated from the faces all around.

In front of Bellingham City Hall the wide street block was so jammed that other phalanxes we couldn't even see waited on side streets a block or so away. A calm, busy policeman delegated to Bill the task of holding the bigger of those side-street crowds until there was room for them to join the main line after it got moving. What a wonderful day to be needed by your home town! Bill said it took a full hour after the march began for everyone to get onto the march route—it felt like everyone in the Bellingham area was either in the march or cheering us on from the sidelines.

But by the second annual Women's March, the news of a national leadership at odds with each other saddened me. I might have chalked up the discord to some normal failure of large groups of volunteeers to hold it together in unity for more than a short time. But there were reports of conflict tinged with racial friction. I didn't suspect that differing religious backgrounds might be a factor in Black and white women's not understanding each other's point of view on the marches, on feminism. Then an article by Eboni Turman in *The Christian Century* caught my eye, and a long-held assumption cracked and tinkled into a heap like a busted window. Even though I pretty much knew that in mainstream books and news, feminism had been centered on the white middle class, feminism was *not* essentially the same among Black women as among white. The complexities of Black women's and white women's relationships are finally reaching secular awareness—I'm glad that feminism can interrogate itself and grow, whatever it comes to be called—but this article went right to the depths by exposing the theological problems between white and Black women.

Black women writers and theologians were ready and waiting to bowl me over. They have things to say, from decades ago, that are vital for white Christian would-be allies to listen to. The 2019 essay I read carried the title, "Black women's faith, black women's flourishing." In it, Turman, of Yale Divinity School, gives a short history of Black women's Christian thinking, starting with a term I was unfamiliar with that came from Alice Walker. Walker, famous as the author of *The Color Purple*, also wrote *In Search of Our Mothers' Gardens: Womanist Prose*. Walker suggested this term, womanist, as better supporting Black women's reality than the term feminism. She was reflecting on a deep sisterhood among women in historically Black churches since at least 1950.

Because of Turman's essay, I sought out a title by Jacquelyn Grant, the first Black woman, Turman says, ever to earn a Ph.D. in systematic theology. My local library searched for a copy of this 1989 book and found one in Claremont, California. It's for scholars, but the title grabbed me: *White Women's Christ and Black Women's Jesus: Feminist Christology and Womanist Response*. Womanist thinking emerged out of decades of Black women supporting and celebrating each other in church. These were the insights I had not been privy to. I'd seen only the legendary Sunday hats and even bigger potlucks of Black church women. But I had wondered about historically Black churches—are they better grounded than predominantly white churches? Not that they would be all alike, but how are they negotiating the complexity of today's Black demographic?—their presence in all economic groups, and the delicacy of Black women supporting Black men against racial discrimination while also pushing back about women's equality.

Womanist thought challenged both white *and Black* theologians. The male model of religious experience simply won't do. And central to this theological literature is the meaning of Jesus' suffering and death for the Black community. Among the topics: white-authored atonement theories.

The atonement theories that had made me so uncomfortable—they were of course created by white men and I'd never considered the implications for Black women. I soaked up the womanist case presented by Turman, including: " . . . [Delores S.] Williams argued that Jesus' suffering does not save black women. To venerate the blood of the cross is to glorify surrogacy—the idea that the suffering of one allows for the redemption of many. Because black women have historically been surrogates, to glorify surrogacy is to regard black women's subjection as sacred. Black women have stood in the place of others, domestically and otherwise, for centuries." No one would question that Black women have suffered because of this status. Yet atonement theory, Turman reports, "has led to deeper pathologizing of black women's lives. To glorify the cross of Jesus [as a redemptive tool] is to glorify suffering. Williams argues that black women carry enough crosses to know that there is no glory in suffering. Instead, Williams emphasized Jesus' 'life and ministerial vision,' calling followers of Christ into a resistance that engenders, and buoys, black women's survival and quality of life."[1]

That must have taken guts for Williams to write, though Turman doesn't mention that. And in the nineteen eighties, no less. I wondered how Williams's words could possibly land well on women heavily invested in the old theology, given that the church has also been a major, huge source of their comfort and strength. I was floored to find such daring, assured thought so buried in an out-of-circulation book. Of course, I was helped to find it by Turman's essay bringing it all back into the here and now.

Turman also examines the Genesis story of the discarded and exiled Hagar. This is the story in which Hagar and her infant son, fathered by Abraham in holiness because Sarah couldn't have children, were turned out of Abraham's house when Sarah became pregnant after all. In the story, God then promised Hagar and her son survival, while promising Sarah's offspring greatness. This fact of the story I didn't like but uneasily accepted, I guess because the marital union is always favored over concubinage. But in this case Abraham's union with Hagar was fully sanctioned as a way to have an heir—So, what gives? Her voice is not present.

The biggest thrill for me was in finding the boldness of these women theologians, paring away the tenets that have grown up around Jesus into a Christology. Women, I'll say it again, were boldly pushing into progressive theology in a way that would ultimately benefit all. I can only guess at the push-back they got. And what a debt progressives owe them.

1. Turman, "Black Women's Faith," para 14.

On women's equality, how far into Christianity can I push? I want to hear there is Christian theology that explicitly acknowledges women's equality with men *and* overrides the apparent contradictions in New Testament texts. I'm glad I asked. Virginia Ramey Mollenkott, the late (white) professor emeritus of William Patterson University, New Jersey, is included in Jacquelyn Grant's literature review and thesis about womanism. Mollenkott was one who distinguished between two kinds of Pauline letters (the letters attributed to the Apostle Paul). One kind addressed "specific church problems which were cultural and time-bound" and therefore not theological (such as the books of 1 Timothy and 1 Corinthians). The other kind has passages such as Galatians 3:28, which famously says, "There is no longer Jew or Greek, there is no longer slave or free, there is no longer male and female; for all of you are one in Christ Jesus." To Mollenkott it is the fact that this latter statement is unbound to time or place that makes it theological.

Like everyone else, I saw "The Color Purple" when the movie came out. While I liked it, at the time I thought it was exaggerated, over the top, to show that Black women's mistreatment could come from Black men as well as white men and women. Now I feel differently. From author Toni Morrison we've heard that Black women's lives could, indeed, be too terrible to talk about. But silence has led to erasure. No wonder white women, would-be allies like me, have so often been inadequate, clueless. The novel *The Color Purple*, now that I have finally read it on the page, makes the abuse of women by men believable in a way that the Hollywood movie did not for me.

More important, even through the horror (and the beautiful writing kept me in it when I might have turned away), Walker refuses to permanently segregate people by good and bad, instead showing redemption coming from wisdom hard earned. Such that a long-sundered intimate relationship could find reconciliation. Not a story of you blew it, buddy, and I survived and found a new man. Walker's story is miles away from the memes of so many movies in our secular society, movies that narrowly center on good women with bad men, or fantasy heroic battles between good men and evil ones. *Purple* the novel is so worth finding and celebrating.

The womanists are brave enough to assert that God's forgiveness is enough without throwing in proxy atonement. Somewhere I picked this up: it was thought Christianity needed a doctrine of original sin in order to make sin big enough to match the gigantic atonement of the crucifixion of the Son of God. Whether or not this particular story of theological reasoning is true, it warns us that each doctrinal decision can lead to another. Barnacles grow. And some really like the build-up of Christology. Fine, maybe, but I like seeing the magnificent whale of Christian faith beneath its barnacle coating.

Surely the doctrine of original sin, that people are born bad, has done a lot of harm. The womanists have looked closely at the consequences of Christian thinking's landing on original sin—how this doctrine resulted in the ugly layered-on anti-woman theology. Original sin stems from a woman, and women are to be forever demoted. Which doesn't make any sense, but how many inanities about women have developed a currency in our society?

It is worth stating clearly that Christian leaders didn't get this idea from Judaism. Original sin is a concept utterly foreign to Judaism. Instead, Rabbi Glickman says, "We see human beings as being born innocent. A sin is something that we *do*, not something that we *are*." (Personal communication with Rabbi Glickman.) I wonder if my mother, all those years ago when she broke off an engagement over her intended's Christian belief about babies going to Hell, had her own rabbi, or channeled one.

In her article, Turman outlines how womanist thinking in recent years has continued to broaden and evolve, and to extend inclusion to Black women who aren't Christian. I was especially interested in discussions insisting that theology must undergird not just surviving, but flourishing—among Black women and in whole communities. Even in their own churches many practices over the years have been a drag on their progress. To mention an important one: exclusion from pastoral and lay leadership, as they often have been, yes, in Black churches, Turman says. Yet it is now obvious to me that in this white-dominated society, Black women must carry on their struggle without pushing down Black men. That's the nuance that Alice Walker achieved in *The Color Purple*.

Now, I need to say I respect those, of any color or locale, who hold on to their inherited version of Christianity. I celebrate the story in the movie, "Lilies of the Field"—the marooned German nuns glory in their new chapel (they pronounce it "shapel,"), their tall wooden cross, stained glass, and lovingly tatted linens for Mass. And I respect those who have tucked away the bothersome within their faith, and I respect those who have walked away altogether. But I personally feel a tremendous sense of liberation in seeing what others have shone a light on, questioned, and peeled away from the tenets of the faith. To my mind, they have given us the teacher Jesus, and a strong and challenging basis for faith for us moderns.

I no longer assume similarities between Black women's and white women's experiences. I feel the humility of having heard other voices. Native women are also calling out their truth in yet another feminism. All I know is I want sisterhood. As for men, I'd love to be a support to the kinds of re-imaginings now going on about masculinity; they also have much to gain from the exciting possibilities in a true intimacy of equals.

31: Comedy Within a Tragic Pattern

E ven so, there comes a time for lightening up. Another Easter went by and we arrived at the perennial topic of the Trinity. To me, explaining the Trinity is the most arcane theological exercise of them all, how three are one, and one of them is both God and human, and there is no hierarchy, or maybe there is with God on top. Not a promising topic on a Sunday when I wanted rest rather than a game of Twister.

I was ready for a mental rest because the previous days had been filled to the brim: a sister-in-law's death, preparations for travel and a gathering, as well as the relatives who arrived here in Bellingham for our grand-nephew's concert. Add the tumble taken by Mom, and at the same time the scramble to accommodate delivery of a hundred-pound toilet (water saver!) and how to get this one-piecer, in its box, up the stairs. After the effort getting it up the stairs we opened the box. The toilet had arrived broken. Quite a week.

Strolling back and forth in front of the pews rather than looking down from the pulpit, Davi had no intention of a theological game of Twister. Our rescue came with simple-silly slides inspired by a group calling themselves Lutheran Satire. They'd made a video about how, in church history, one misstep or loose use of an analogy got one into hot water. The attempts over time to explicate the Trinity, and the wrathful accusations of heresy these attempts called forth— I just shake my head at how long this tug-of-war went on. "St. Patrick's Bad Analogies" was indeed good for a laugh, and also instructive about theological wrangling.

With equal lightness, Kent had often said from the pulpit: "If you believe that a little, or if you believe that a lot, say Amen!" I think humor is a fine way to deal with a religious history chock full of power fights masquerading as discernment of truth. I can only wish that early church fathers had managed to hold strong on the equality of women that, to my reading, Christianity started with in its revolutionary days. Very convenient, isn't it, that the boys' clubs and their arcane power struggles long kept men too busy to consider women, except to box them in, and make women a too-easy target whenever a target is needed for blame-throwing. I cannot forget that women were still, in the 1800s, being told to wait for the basic right to vote, some men habitually flogging the specious argument that there were more important issues to settle first. It can't be surprising that the subjection of women, a many-faceted tragedy in culture at-large, would be reflected also in the Church, and need to be resisted there, too.

32: A Human Place, a Gutsy Place.
A Place for Me.

This is a very human place after all, this church. Pastor Sharon's prayer one Sunday reminded us that church multiplies our celebrations and divides our sorrows. I'd seen it borne out in a concrete, here-and-now way. I'd had my disappointments, with the coal neutrality, paper usage, and Justice at the Table. But my personal disappointment that church members weren't more gung-ho to join my projects didn't give the lie to all the supportive things they *did* do for me, including all who made "my" picnic work out. At a low point I once wondered if church was just a social club with spiritual benefits. Not that that would be worthless. But a church is perfectly positioned in our society to be much more than that: to be a small, close-knit, spiritually rich village within so much urban anonymity. Or within rural isolation, though coastal urban cities are what I know. I don't want to cultivate spirituality as only a solo pursuit, not anymore. Give me a face-to-face community of spiritual travelers any day.

Is what I found locally just a rarity in this age, as we're told, of mainline church decline? Maybe not. Church history scholar and public theologian Diana Butler Bass criss-crossed the country for a study of churches to find what seems to make some of them flourish. She found that the neighborhood church is alive, and some of them are very well, indeed. "Strands of American Christianity have long resisted [the] temptation to theological narrowness and instead emphasized intellectual openness as a practice of faith. This tradition of inquiry has generally been called liberal Protestantism, a theological movement going back to the sixteenth century that emphasizes the free conscience of the individual in matter of faith against all forms of authoritarianism. . . . Once, not so long ago, *liberal* was a good word meaning generosity and openness. It implied a host of positive things: reform, freedom, toleration, thoughtful inquiry, and lack of prejudice and absence of bigotry. In its most classical sense, liberal meant opposition to dogmatism, authoritarianism, inquisition, religious bigotry, and theological intolerance. Historically, religious liberality—theological generosity—sparked much of the energy, passion, and intellectual liveliness of American Protestantism."[1]

At the personal level as I look back at my original hopes in coming to the church I joined, I recall my wish to replace the social bonds and belonging of my job, and maybe find more peace within myself. I am not doing badly on either. Even a submerged wish for a fuller healing from the wounds of my first marriage has been fulfilled. And the patterns of my responses to disappointments and obstacles have changed. I have more patience and compassion for my husband's patterns as well as my own, though I am still no saint and won't ever be. There is no denying what a progressive new light shining on church membership did for me. And for my outlook on world religions. Ironically, this progressivism is deeply conservative of Christian origins, and of the revolutionary Jesus. He would never have allied himself with a Roman Empire, then or in its modern equivalents. Can you doubt that? It is beautiful that I no longer have to put an entire American spiritual river away from me. This fills me with hope. This is far more than I'd dreamed when I set out.

But I had yet more to discover, about gutsiness.

The work to make this Congregational church open and affirming started long before I joined, and some of the work may have been discouragingly hard and slow. Even years later, in 2016 after we also supported marriage equality, some hellfire picketers ringed our parking lot shouting the name of the place in the afterlife to which we were surely consigned. We must be doing something right. We must be doing something valuable. Not just treading water, as I worried. I guess I figured that particular fight was over

1. Butler Bass, *Christianity for the Rest of Us*, 190.

and we should be adopting a big new initiative. But standing together and smiling back at the loud picketers was a re-celebration of sorts.

One Saturday not long after the picketers incident, Bill and I headed to the farmers market. A familiar man was posted on his usual corner with his tall sign ("All men shall kneel . . ."), a real shouter, seeming to enjoy carrying on for maximum annoyance, a man who later made a quixotic run for city council. This Saturday, on a whim, I went up to him and asked him what church he belonged to. He admitted he didn't belong to any church, he just knew what he knew about hellfire and damnation, and he "knew" that gay people are all among the damned. That's curious, I thought. All you had to do, according to your placard, was accept Jesus. I didn't say that to him. I'd said enough with my first question.

FCCB was about to do another big thing. The strong current of desire about using our big church building to serve our community in a bigger way had now been percolating for years. Wonderful concerts, often fundraisers, were already a fixture in the acoustically fine Sanctuary. Various community support groups met regularly in the classrooms downstairs, and we'd opened our doors for special forums. We'd hosted Black Lives Matter and other groups. But this strong desire was not satisfied. We still had a large unfinished space in the downstairs basement, unfinished but nice—some daylight, and most assuredly not a dirt floor like in the long-ago church building. Little used, especially after the annual charity rummage sale was sunsetted. The space seemed to languish, with stored goods stacked here and there and lots of unused space. Finally the percolator erupted with a really big partnership. Northwest Youth Services (NWYS) would use the space for aid and respite for young homeless people. Or, as we say, those who are experiencing homelessness, so as not to reinforce homelessness as part of their very identity.

How did such a partnership come about? A member of FCCB was on the board of NWYS. He was boggled to learn that 40 percent of the young people NWYS served in the previous year were on the street only because they'd been rejected by their own religious families, some because of non-cisgender orientations. It became clear that we are called to this project, and not only because we have space.

Entering into this partnership with Northwest Youth Services will mean major costs to prepare the space in order to have showers, washing machines, lounge and meeting and program space, a kitchen, a little library. Permanent staff, and liaisons to services including school counselors and other resources round out the list. Approved by a vote of the congregation—it is said that courage is fear that has said its prayers—the project will be called the Ground Floor. As the project came to seem real, an enormous capital campaign gathered steam, and I and the rest of the congregation have jumped into fundraising and commitment at a scale that I would have found extremely daunting just a few months earlier. Cash-limited, I sold my gold jewelry, and it felt like I was back in the canoe surfing a standing wave yelling, "Woo-hoo!"

This is a form of place saving, though it looks quite different from the permaculture of that Mennonite group. Greater use for an existing building. A hand up for the next generation of adult workers and leaders who will be on the front lines of our response to climate destruction.

With that decision made, and perhaps now that our fears about opening up our basement have been largely answered, we are busted open in other ways, too. Sharon, along with Davi and Sharry, and Deanna staying part-time—seem to be able to juggle multiple issues with steady hands. Or maybe Sharon is more accepting than Kent had been of letting the church either grow or not, by the entirety of its lights. Maybe if the coal problem had come now, official reactions would have been different. No matter. For the Ground Floor, Davi has led outreach into the neighborhood, crucial work that is helping allay some anxiety about the new thing coming to their backyard. We say our prayers, but we also listen to our neighbors.

This big project wasn't enough for some of us. Before the various Ground Floor project committees—communications and education, fundraising, construction design and planning, and so forth—could tell us in detail what we faced, another project proposal whip-sawed me, now on the Mission and Justice Board. Inter-Faith Coalition asked FCCB to be one of thirteen churches in a new program to take turns housing and feeding homeless families for a week at a time. The program, called Family Promise, was begun by conservative churches elsewhere. Champions of Family Promise in our congregation rushed this new idea to the Mission and Justice. I missed that particular meeting, and when the draft minutes arrived in my email, it looked as if they had approved it on the spot. This set me to worrying, my specialty. They were rushing something that would gobble up an enormous amount of the volunteer capacity of the church—thirty FCCB volunteers were called for. It turned out that others at the meeting felt it hadn't really, actually, finally been approved, but approved for further discussion. At the next meeting, we held more of a debate, asking if we wanted to just pick up the slack for anti-poor governmental budget cuts, versus pushing for positive policies that would *prevent* homelessness. But in the end, the group preferred to jump at the chance to catch a precious few families falling into homelessness.

Those of us who were concerned about over-stretching our volunteers weren't exactly wrong—the calls for volunteers for the baseline necessaries of coffee time, ushers, greeters, boards, even a church treasurer, have become harder to fill and sometimes filled at the last moment.

Still, I came to appreciate the Family Promise project. An observer from outside of our church told me he has since seen signs of softening in some of the most hard-shelled churches that are interacting with us. These are churches who have habitually steered clear of working with anyone who didn't see Christianity exactly as they did. And, indeed, they didn't much care for the program rule against proselytizing. Yet now they are willing partners and friendly with us. At FCCB as well, we've seen benefits from hosting Family Promise, including helping us integrate new members eager to have something planned and concrete to jump into. Maybe I'm also learning something more about the Zanderses' *The Art of Possibility*. Any of us can lead from where we sit, as they say, but enrolling others, as they also say, in one's passion projects sometimes means being willing to enroll in theirs.

On a recent Sunday, Sharon said that you can't predict who or what will bear fruit. She was talking about the Parable of the Sower, which is usually taken to mean seed must fall on good, prepared soil to flourish, and usually those in the pews (from my past experience) get exhorted to prepare themselves, be good soil for God's work. But Sharon, subversively, told of a pastor who tried to prove the parable to his flock, and learned something. You may recall how the parable goes: some seed fell on the path, and the birds scarfed it up. Some on the rocks, where the soil was shallow and the harsh sun killed the sprouts because they had little root. Some fell into the choking thorns, and last, some fell onto good promising soil. Well, in the instance Sharon recounted, the pastor sowed actual, not metaphoric, bean seed. Much of it sprouted, but after four weeks the bean plant in the thorns was the only one that remained. Make of that what you will. I loved it. Maybe someone rescued from homelessness will emerge as a leader in systemic change permitting others to thrive.

How do churches adopt a new thing and de-emphasize an old one? As in government, or in the economy, or in dentistry, we are never starting from square one, *tabula rasa*, genesis. If we are always dealing with structures and strictures that once served better than they do now, how do we change without tearing the proverbial fabric of shared beliefs and expectations? That's what society wrestles with. Christian denominations have undergone alterations, small and large, progressive and regressive. For Protestants, the mother of them all was the cataclysmic Protestant Reformation, yet seemingly smaller changes also have had big effects. In *Saving Jesus from the Church*, Robin Meyers, in recounting Borg's work researching the four meanings of the term faith, says that "only one of them, *assensus*, has anything to do with intellectual assent . . ." It was only over time that the meaning of orthodoxy shifted from, as Meyers says, "correct worship" to "right belief." So what would we expect after modern science challenged the most literal of biblical worldviews? In a sizable portion of Christian denominations "faith has come to mean believing things that are increasingly easy to disprove."[2]

The late paleontologist and essayist Stephen Jay Gould traced the genesis of the "warfare model of science and religion" to an 1870s fight, and interestingly, not before. Even medieval religious scholars were not flat-earthers. Gould's book, *Rocks of Ages: Science and Religion in the Fullness of Life* is a lovely read about science and religion as distinct "magisteria."[3] Religious history really does begin to sound like earthquake records—stress building up until bump, it get released, only to build up again and head toward another break, even changing the placement of river channels. But in religion what was done can be undone, with a caveat.

I don't think progressives can change things for conservative churches. That hard paddling will have to be done from inside. I celebrate rustlings of change in the most fortressed evangelicalism. I think of the late Rachel Held Evans, daughter of a minister. You won't find her work in the nationally carried noise. Yet, as is so often the case, where there is a closed and well-defended subculture, change eventually comes from the inside. Evans may be the exemplar, for the strictest evangelicals, of a speaker for change coming from within the ranks, and actually getting traction. In her short life she braved a good deal of hostility for her views on women's roles and how a religion needs to be able to evolve. But she tapped a silent and hungry following, those afraid to say anything within their face-to-face circles, but only too thrilled to find a voice for their doubts and distress

2. Meyers, *Saving Jesus*, 37.
3. Gould, *Rocks of Ages*, 118.

through her words on the Internet and in her books. We progressives can offer evangelicals as much compassion as we can muster for their pain, and yes, for their anger. Other than that, I see myself continuing on with my river journey, doing what we progressives can do.

For progressives, letting our faith breathe, and float, might have meant throwing old texts overboard, but I'm glad it hasn't. We can keep, and increasingly appreciate, what is ancient. Especially I'm glad Hebrew scriptures are in the Christian Bible. One of the happy results of my quest was that I was gaining an ever-increasing appreciation for Judaism that I admit I'd never had before. The Biblical Hebrew scriptures blossomed for me when I was invited to consider the overall movement from the older books to the later ones. I had looked at the books in that tremendous, frustrating and perplexing library as separate texts often competing or contradicting each other. As if each prescription and proscription, each story staked the same ground claiming unchanging truth. Rob Bell, the best-selling author I never heard of but whose *What Is the Bible?* changed my way of seeing these texts. He finds the movement along an arc rather than looking at each part alone. Interestingly, non-church-going Bill is the one who brought home this book. Bell finds an arc in how the ancient Israelites thought of the divine and of themselves. Going back to the early books of the Hebrew scriptures, Bell asks us to compare the giant contrast between Judaic conceptions and ancient Greek thought. How selfish, unpredictable, and downright petulant the Greek gods were, and how this view wasn't unique—many groups had similar conceptions of gods in very ancient times. Now imagine a steady and loving God. In the context of their times, ancient Israelites made a giant seismic shift, breaking from those around them. Further along, these people of Judah were given work to do—another seismic shift—imagine a calling to a new covenant to bless all mankind.

Being chosen had ultimately nothing to do with excluding others. This is huge and beautiful.

It shook me when I realized I had quietly, beneath the level of active thought, held a view of Judaism as being superseded by Christianity. I now can see the destructiveness of that view. I now see Judaism as the vital and complete-in-itself religion it is—Christianity's older sibling—as alive and true today as it was when followers of Jesus created something new. I wish I could have my friend Corine back, my high school friend who made many trips between California and Washington with the cat who enjoyed car travel. Corine converted to Judaism in her later years. I never talked with her about her conversion because I was so nonplussed for anything to say or ask. Now she's gone.

If churches can change, can repair the messes that turn away spiritual seekers, they can take a crucial place in this increasingly elbow-to-elbow, unsettled world. The most difficult lift for some, I have to believe, will concern a way-back notion, the one that says there is only one correct religious story, immutable and infallible for all time. This notion has worn threadbare from constant chafing as peoples have been shoved closer and closer together, but it still retains enough strength to hang many up. To some Christian leaders, even to entertain discussion, or any reinterpretation, is to invite things to fall apart utterly.

Even so, if the major Christian leader Brian D. McLaren is right, it won't be long before the bulk of Christianity turns like a flock of birds. And, by the way, his background is evangelical. In the church library I found his *The Great Spiritual Migration*. Subtitled *How the World's Largest Religion is Seeking a Better Way to be Christian*, he believes that churches can fairly easily get past the exclusivity of one right set of beliefs. He bases this belief in part on Eastlake Community Church in Bothell, Washington, where they embrace something more transformational as well as more humble than we-are-right churches. In checking out their website, it looks as if they've attracted lots of younger adults, in itself a hopeful development.

I admit it is hard to picture how some national church leaders can contemplate the unthinkable, especially those who circle the swelling lake of religious nationalism. Still, reality can eventually gobsmack leaders and followers alike. Often youth will lead. Here in the U.S., one by one, churches are finding a new story of contributions by everyone, with leaders as likely to be women as men, or LBGTQ+. Young people, even in conservative churches, are refusing to exclude LBGTQ friends. As to climate disasters and respect for our home, our places, our natural life-supports, I can hope the blinkered churches will take to heart a 2016 book by one of their own, addressing their own evangelical values: *Caring for Creation: An Evangelical's Guide to Climate Change and a Healthy Environment*, by the popular Minnesota meteorologist Paul Douglas. It connects the dots for them and proclaims it is pro-life to protect God's creation, further reminding readers of the connection between protecting the Earth and protecting children from pollution-inflamed illnesses such as asthma.

I also wonder if conservative churches might be able to see themselves mirrored in a far-away place. Some ancient Hindu texts, for example, advise people to relieve themselves far from home, according to a 2014 article in the *New York Times*, titled "Malnutrition in Well-Fed Children Is Linked to Poor Sanitation." Spending $26 billion on food and jobs programs and less than $400 million on sanitation, India has found that they can't get there from here. Open defecation away from home just fouls someone else's home, and they of course foul yours. So now, or as of 2014, half of India drinks from contaminated water. Too many of India's children are stunted mentally and physically—no matter how much good food they get—from being sick so often from fecal contamination in their water. So far, even when toilets are provided, they are not always used.[4] It will take some time for doctrines and practices to shift. Change they must, eventually. If they don't, their fate is another stagnant lake behind a dam, and the world will move right around them. After we have a laugh over World Toilet Day (it's in November) we should hope the world will help India in this.

All of our problems will take patience. Long term, we need blind patience, for we may not live to see much progress. That leap can be aided by being in a faith community. How much faithful patience is needed? My hope for any breakthroughs on climate pollution led me to eagerly read "What It Takes to Clean the Ganges," by George Black. We all know how woefully polluted the Ganges River is. I hoped for good news in the article about cleaning it up. Nothing is straightforward in India, however, and the story was about interfaith conflict and indifference. But at the end of the article, Black interviews a man, Navneet Raman, who "reached into a bag and scooped out a handful of shiny purple seeds the size of pistachios. They were seeds of the tropical almond, *Terminalia catappa*, and would grow into what is known locally as 'the sewage tree,' because it can filter heavy metals and other pollutants out of standing water." Raman told Black, "Most people come to Benares to pay last respects to the memory of their near and dear ones who have passed away. So I thought that on this bank of the river we could make a forest of remembrance. This is my guerrilla warfare." Raman's vision for the future includes gardens, walkways, and shaded benches. Black asked him if he ever became discouraged by the slow pace of change. He shrugged and said that all he can do is place his trust in Shiva. "India is a land of discouragement. If you're not discouraged by the harsh summers, then you are discouraged by the cow eating your plant, or the motorbike or tractor or car that is running over your plant, or the neighbor who is

4. Harris, "Malnutrition in Well-Fed Children," A1.

plucking the leaves from it just for fun as he is going by. If you can't deal with discouragement, India has no place for you."[5]

If that isn't a story of religious faithfulness, then what is? I return to humming the Thew Elliott hymn that seemed to call me even before I was introduced to it. Christianity is never going to be perfect for everyone or all needs. Maybe the call is more important than finding perfection. Like housework, a faith is never done, complete. A work in progress, adapting, growing, changing. Not even *a* work. Not a *thing*, no matter how beautiful it can be. A way. A way of living, of being.

I see no need to view religion like eating one's vegetables. Though I happen to like vegetables. Religion, in a supportive church, synagogue, or mosque, is about getting along with each other and living joyfully. My quest has proven one of Alain de Botton's insights in *Religion for Atheists*—that in secular society communal joy can only happen in special circumstances. Like we'd experienced in the women's marches of 2017. But a church community has a leg up on communal joy over and over again, or can if it so chooses.

About the time that my story closes, in the social hall for an evening potluck marking some occasion, we again sang "Draw the Circle Wide." This time, the words that had brought me to bitter tears after my Justice at the Table flop, became joyful again for me. A physician by the friendly name of Pete took my hand as we stood in a circle. And I thought that the same things that have gone wrong with Christianity—the same patterns— are evident in our culture at large, and in human nature and human politics, and human workplaces. And things go right, as well. I'm glad I got the chance to renew my bonds with my faith community. And I'm glad I went further back, into my cultural inheritance. Simply withdrawing from associations because I can find fault with them only shrinks my world. Here in church as well as with family and friends, I can enjoy the bonds with less stress and less politics than elsewhere. Moreover, as author McLaren says: "I discovered at a young age that although you can learn beliefs in isolation, you can't learn love apart from a community."[6]

If I had simply visited my progressive church a while and quit again, I'd still have come away happier for reclaiming a place for Christianity to rest comfortably in my mind. Happier for clearing out my locked cupboard, for learning more about love, for being able to see all stripes of Christians

5. Black, "What It Takes."

6. McLaren, *Great Migration*, 56.

with new eyes. It's simply good to know a kinder yet more challenging Christianity exists and may be growing and sweetening the world. The church became one fewer of American disappointments. That would have been a nourishing cargo of riches on its own. But I stayed.

Maybe you can't step into the same river twice. But in another sense, the river I stuck my toe in those dozen years ago is still the same—refreshing, and buoyant under a boat for shooting the rapids. And won't it be great when our church's daylight basement is built out and young people can find respite there from homelessness, respite even from rejection, and maybe they'll find new security and opportunity. Perhaps we can help these young people recognize that they, too, have much to contribute.

My paddle catches a wave and gives me hope for a new climate justice task group Davi will help me lead. Sharon puts words to what I now know about triumphs and failures: She and her father "shared the journey in different ways at different times . . . When you have a head of steam to 'move through' and others don't, then ask for their prayers to see you through. But we don't stop there." No, we don't stop there.

I say Amen.

Bibliography

Bell, Rob. *What Is the Bible? How an Ancient Library of Poems, Letters, and Stories Can Transform the Way You Think and Feel About Everything.* New York: HarperOne, 2017.

Black, George. "What It Takes to Clean the Ganges." *New Yorker* 92 (July 25, 2016). https://www.newyorker.com/magazine/2016/07/25/what-it-takes-to-clean-the-gangesonline.

Borg, Marcus. *Speaking Christian: Why Christian Words Have Lost Their Meaning and Power—And How They Can Be Restored.* New York: HarperOne, 2011.

Borg, Marcus, and John Crossan. *The Last Week: A Day-by-Day Account of Jesus's Final Week in Jerusalem.* San Francisco: Harper Collins, 2006.

Butler Bass, Diana. *Christianity for the Rest of Us: How the Neighborhood Church is Transforming the Faith.* SanFrancisco: HarperCollins, 2006.

Coffey, Michael. "Palm or Passion, Wave or Particle." In *Mystery Without Rhyme or Reason: Poetic Reflections on the Revised Common Lectionary,* 143–44. Eugene, OR: Wipf & Stock, 2015.

Colker, David. "The Rev. Everett Parker, Who Fought a TV Station's Racism, Dies at 102." *Los Angeles Times,* September 23, 2015.

Denherder-Thomas, Timothy. "The Heart of Climate Justice: Creating the Energy Infrastructure We Want to See." *Humanist,* July 2, 2019. https://thehumanist.com/magazine/july-august-2019/features/climate-justice-the-minnesota-model-for-building-a-better-future-for-us-all.

Geering, Lloyd. "A Venerable New Church." *The Fourth R* 30 (2017) 7–23.

Glock, Charles Y., et al. *To Comfort and to Challenge: A Dilemma of the Contemporary Church.* Berkeley: University of California Press, 1967.

Gould, Stephen Jay. *Rocks of Ages: Science and Religion in the Fullness of Life.* New York: Ballantine, 1999.

Grant, Jacquelyn. *White Women's Christ and Black Women's Jesus: Feminist Christology and Womanist Response.* American Academy of Religion Academy Series 64. Atlanta, GA: Scholars, 1989.

Halley, Henry Hampton. *Halley's Bible Handbook® An Abbreviated Bible Commentary.* 24th ed. Grand Rapids: Zondervan, 1965.

Harris, Gardiner. "Malnutrition in Well-Fed Children Is Linked to Poor Sanitation." *New York Times,* July 15, 2014, Section A1.

Kershner, Isabel, and Halbfinger, David M. "Israelis Reflect on Gaza: 'I Hope at Least That Each Bullet Was Justified.'" *New York Times,* May 16, 2018, Section A1.

Lamott, Anne. *Traveling Mercies: Some Thoughts on Faith.* New York: Anchor, 2000.

McLaren, Brian D. *The Great Spiritual Migration: How the World's Largest Religion is Seeking a Better Way to be Christian.* New York: Convergent, 2016.

Meyers, Robin. *Saving Jesus from the Church: How to Stop Worshipping Christ and Start Following Jesus.* New York: HarperOne, 2009.

Miles, Sara. *Take This Bread: A Radical Conversion.* New York: Ballantine, 2007.

Murray, Keith A. *Centennial Churches of Washington's "Fourth Corner."* Occasional Paper #20, Bellingham: Center for Pacific Northwest Studies, Western Washington University, 1985.

Myers, Ched. "Permeneutics!" *Ched Meyers* (blog), May 9, 2014. https://chedmyers.org/2014/05/09/blog-2014-05-09-permeneutics/.

Norris, Kathleen. *Amazing Grace: A Vocabulary of Faith.* New York: Riverhead, 1998.

Pagels, Elaine. *Adam, Eve, and the Serpent.* New York: Random House, 1988.

Papanikolaou, Aristotle. "How I Teach Theology to Undergrads." *Christian Century*, February 6, 2017. https://www.christiancentury.org/article/features/how-i-teach-theology-undergrads.

Pederson, Rena. *The Lost Apostle: Searching for the Truth About Junia.* San Francisco: Jossey-Bass, 2006.

Prather, Hugh. *Notes on How to Live in the World . . . and Still Be Happy.* New York: Doubleday, 1986.

Remnick, David. *The Devil Problem, and Other True Stories.* New York: Random, 1996.

Struckmeyer, Kurt. "The Words of the Eucharist." *Progressive Christianity* (February 5, 2016). https://progressivechristianity.org/resources/the-words-of-the-eucharist/.

Tarrant, John. *Bring Me the Rhinoceros, And Other Zen Koans to Bring You Joy.* New York: Harmony, 1997.

Turman, Eboni Marshall. "Black Women's Faith, Black Women's Flourishing: A Critical Essay." *Christian Century* 136 (February 28, 2019). https://christiancentury.org/article/critical-essay/black-women-s-faith-black-women-s-flourishing.

Wade, Nicholas. "A Fragile Text Gets a Virtual Read." *New York Times,* Jan. 9, 2018, D3.

Zander, Rosamund Stone, and Benjamin Zander. *The Art of Possibility: Transforming Professional and Personal Life.* Boston: Harvard Business School Press, 2000.

CPSIA information can be obtained
at www.ICGtesting.com
Printed in the USA
LVHW071409140623
749737LV00004B/151